I0090361

Praise for the Dating Goddess

The *Adventures in Delicious Dating After 40* series of books is based on the blog Adventures in Delicious Dating After 40 at www.DatingGoddess.com. Here are comments from readers.

♥ "Adventures in Delicious Dating After 40 is a wonderful composite of both the mechanics of post-40 online dating and what the practice of honoring one's self actually looks like. How marvelous your writing is to read. I spent about 2 hours reading and was riveted the whole time." —Maggie Hanna

♥ "At last, a dating writer who addresses requirements. You are SO right on! I'm thrilled to have found you!" —Rachel Sarah, author, *Single Mom Seeking*

♥ "Powerfully heartfelt and honest writing. You are inspiring." —Kare Anderson, Emmy Award winning writer

"I just love your writing. It is very fresh and gives the reader something to think about." — Kelly Lantz, President & Manager, 55-Alive.com

"Dating Goddess, you are like a, a, a, well, a goddess to me. You've helped guide me successfully through my re-entry into the dating world after 14 years. I'm an eager student and fast study, and do get myself into situations that others don't know how to deal with — such as 3 dates in one day -— so thankfully you are there! You're the greatest, thanks for all you do for us!" —Jae G.

"I find your point of view much more interesting than other dating writers. Thanks for always reminding me to enjoy dating life no matter what it throws at you." —Sandy

"I love Adventures in Delicious Dating After 40. I really do like your honest and authentic voice — it's refreshing." —Wendy S.

"Adventures in Delicious Dating After 40 is really fun to read. Thanks for sharing your thoughts and letting us divorced single women know that we are not alone. There's a lot here that I identify with, although I'm not as brave as you are about dating lots of guys. So far. Love your blog — the first blog I've ever read consistently." —Elizabeth

From Fear to Frolic

Getting Naked Without Getting Embarrassed

by Dating Goddess

From Fear to Frolic: Get Naked Without Getting Embarrassed

Second Edition

© 2012 All rights reserved. No part of this book may be reproduced or transmitted in any form or by any means, electronic or mechanical, including photocopying, recording, or by any information storage or retrieval system, without the written permission from the copyright holder, except for the inclusion of quotations in a review.

Cover design by Dave Innis, www.innisanimation.com

Book design by JustYourType.biz

Printed in the United States of America.

ISBN   Print: 978-1-930039-91-9

eBook: 978-1-930039-22-3

How to order:

The *Adventures in Delicious Daing After 40* books may be ordered directly from www.DatingGoddess.com.

Quantity discounts are also available. Visit us online for updates and additional articles.

The Adventures in Delicious Dating After 40 books are dedicated to my ex-husband since he unexpectedly released me to explore the untethered life of a single woman. I then had the freedom for the experiences, lessons and insights shared in these pages.

Books by Dating Goddess

Date or Wait: Are You Ready for Mr. Great?

Assessing Your Assets: Why You're A Great Catch

In Search of King Charming: Who Do I Want to Share My Throne?

Embracing Midlife Men: Insights Into Curious Behaviors

Dipping Your Toe in the Dating Pool: Dive In Without Belly Flopping

Winning at the Online Dating Game: Stack the Deck in Your Favor

Check Him Out Before Going Out: Avoiding Dud Dates

First-Rate First Dates: Increasing the Chances of a Second Date

Real Deal or Faux Beau: Should You Keep Seeing Him?

Multidating Responsibly: Play the Field Without Being A Player

Moving On Gracefully: Break Up Without Heartache

From Fear to Frolic: Get Naked Without Getting Embarrassed

Ironing Out Dating Wrinkles: Work Through Challenges Without Getting Steamed

Contents

viii

Introduction

his book is designed for anyone who is interested in stories, advice, and lessons from the midlife dating front. If you are over 40 and haven't dated in a while — or even if you have — you'll learn ways to approach dating with zeal, optimism, and hope. Even if you've had more than your share of negative experiences, I'll share how to glean lessons from those adventures, rather than just declaring that "all men are jerks" or "men are just looking for sex."

While most of the perspective is from a woman to women, men's comments, experiences, and lessons have been integrated as appropriate.

This book began as daily entries into my blog, Adventures in Delicious Dating After 40, which has been featured in the *Wall Street Journal* as well as on radio and TV. I wrote about my epiphanies from my and my friends' dating life. The best postings were culled to make this and subsequent books.

This book focuses on what you need to consider and know before getting physically intimate with a man you're dating. This is nerve-wracking to many midlife women. This will prepare you.

This book consists of three types of perspectives:

💜 **Lessons:** These are specific experiences I thought would be useful to you. A few lines from my experience illustrate the points.

💜 **Insights:** These usually start with an experience I've encountered, then the insights that experience spawned. It is usually comprised of around half story and half insight.

💜 **Stories:** These are examples of situations I've experienced — or was currently experiencing when I wrote that piece — that I thought would be entertaining. Or I thought the story would help you see what kind of things happen in the midlife dating world so you'd know what has happened to others.

Because these writings were real time, as they occured, they are often set in the present tense. But they are not chronological. So a reference to "my current beau" may now be many sweethearts ago. I hope this isn't confusing.

I'd love ot hear your stories and questions. Please email them to me at Goddess@DatingGoddess.com. They may make it into the blog or my next book!

Who is the Dating Goddess?

I am a middle-aged, white, professional woman. My husband of nearly 20 years left me in April 2003 when I was 47, 11 days shy of 48. After giving my heart time to heal from the surprise divorce sprung by the man I thought was my soulmate, I started dating 18 months later. Generally, I have had a great time meeting interesting men, some of whom became romantic beaus, some became treasured friends, and some I never heard from again.

I am not a well-preserved, gorgeous, marathon-running middle-aged women

In the beginning, I had dates with single male colleagues, but I quickly found Internet dating was the way to explore the most "inventory" and qualify men who I thought might be a good match.

I am not one of those well-preserved, gorgeous,

marathon-running middle-aged women. I have been told I am attractive, but I am overweight and not a gym rat. So while I am active, I do not match the description 90% of men's profiles say they want: slender, athletic, toned, fit. I have some wrinkles — what one sweet suitor mistakenly called dimples. I have what Bridget Jones called "wobbly bits," as most non-surgically enhanced middle-aged women do. My genes — and a lifetime addiction to chocolate — have made their mark. Yet I've met and dated some wonderful men, so even if you're not a lingerie model, you can find guys who will think you're attractive, perhaps even hot!

In my professional life, I am a bestselling author of workplace effectiveness books, professional speaker and management consultant. I've appeared on Oprah, 60 Minutes, and National Public Radio and in the *Wall Street Journal* and *USA Today.*

This book is intended to not only be useful to others and cathartic for me, but is also the genesis of a new topic for fun, thought-provoking speeches. I'm calling myself a dating philosopher and giving date-a-vational speeches! Let me know if you know a group who would like an entertaining after-lunch speech on how lessons learned from dating have implications in business and personal relationships and well as life philosophies.

How did I come by the Dating Goddess moniker? After a few months of dating dozens of men — one week yielded 7 dates with 6 guys in 5 days — my friends dubbed me this name. I liked it, so it stuck.

I'm purposefully not sharing my picture as I don't want you to think either, "How did she get any dates at all?" or the opposite, "Of course she found it easy to get 112 men to ask her out." I am not hideous (usually) nor am I stunning (without professional hair, makeup and Photoshop!). Some men find me attractive, some don't.

I continue to search for my "one," but I have learned a lot along the way, and my single and not-single friends have loudly encouraged me to share my experiences and lessons in the hopes of helping others navigate the adventure of dating with more success. And to have a delicious time doing it!

Make sure to download your free eBook Attract Your Next Great Mate: Dating Advice From Top Relationship Experts at www.Dating-Goddess.com/freebie

Sleepover do's and don'ts

"Sleepover? For adults?" you may be asking. "What do you mean?"

Two-person pajama party. Duo slumber shindig. Couple cuddle fest. Jammie jam. No-sex sleepover. It can happen early in the relationship. You're not ready to have sex, so you only cuddle and snooze with your new sweetie all night.

Sleepovers are living on the edge. There is potential danger. You have to trust the guy enough to know he won't force you to do anything you don't want to do. I'm not advocating them; however, I know they happen. I'll share some guidelines if you decide it is right for you.

When are sleepovers likely to happen? When you've been out on a date until late. Your date brings you home but is exhausted and has a long drive ahead, or he has had a tad too much to drink so is uncomfortable driving. Coffee would barely make a dent in his alertness. He's been a gentleman in every encounter with you. You haven't had to reel him in. He's shown he is trustworthy through his actions and words. He's honored your boundaries.

One option is for him to sleep in the guest room or on the couch. But know that if there are sparks between you, one of you may join the other before morning. More often sleepovers are in the same bed.

One of you may join the other before morning

How tos:

🖤 Explain he can stay, but there will be no sex of any kind. Some people have Clintonian definitions of sex, so be clear you mean *no* sex.

🖤 Clothing is *not* optional. At minimum, undies must stay on, in their proper place (around one's knees does not count as "on," although technically they are on your body). Ideally, you both wear — and keep on—— something non-sexy, e.g., t-shirts and sweat pants, pajamas — tops and bottoms. Flannel or cotton, not silk or satin. The less exposed skin the better, so avoid camisoles. I'm not meaning to sound prudish, but you want to be uninviting in this situation. Don't don your frilly, see-through negligee for a sleepover. Save it for later. It will only invite trouble.

❤ Expect there will be some "exploration" — unless you have a bundling board. It is hard for two attracted people to keep their hands off each other. So verbalize your boundaries and if his hand "slips" reinforce what's OK by moving it as well as restating your boundary. If this "slippage" happens more than a couple of times, kick him out.

❤ You have to stick to your own rules. You can't change midway and say, "You feel so good, let's have sex." You are then sending mixed messages and he won't want to honor your limits in the future because he won't think you're serious about them.

❤ Don't be a temptress to test his mettle. It is hard enough for two people to lie together, so don't let your hand "slip" to a sensitive zone, nor engage in passionate kissing or other provocative behaviors. You are putting him in a double bind and most mortals would not pass the test. Don't do this.

So with all these rules, why do it? And why wouldn't you?

The pros:

❤ You confirm you can trust him to honor your wishes. If you can trust him in the face of temptation, it will deepen the relationship.

💜 There is something delicious about sleeping intertwined with someone you care about.

The cons:

💜 You may not get a lot of sleep. Sleeping with someone new takes some getting used to. It's easy to wake when he turns. He may snore. Sleeping with your head on his chest may sound romantic, but it can create neck pain.

💜 He will be there in the morning, when you'll have morning breath, possibly a hangover, and sans makeup. You may also have to share bathroom time before work, find him a toothbrush and razor, make him breakfast.

Sleepovers are really a matter of trust. For a sleepover to be successful you have to have clearly defined boundaries and confidence in your and his ability to respect them. Be firm in your rules. Don't waffle. When pajama parties work, they are a delicious way to deepen your relationship.

Does he want in your life — or just in your bedroom?

I had a hot and heavy relationship with a man I dated for 5 months. It was one of those instant chemistry situations and after our second date we couldn't keep our hands off each other. We saw each other once a week, sometimes for several days, even though he lived less than an hour away. He always brought me a gift, and in between visits he sent me daily loving text messages, IMs, emails, and/or e-cards. Nothing salacious, just romantic and sweet.

The relationship progressed quickly, something I told myself not to do. But I was so drawn to him, and he to me, it was futile trying to put the brakes on. It seemed we were both falling hard and fast.

I thought he was being a gentleman by always making the journey to my house so I didn't have to drive the hour to his. After a month, I suggested we share the driving burden and meet at his house occasionally. He always had a viable reason this wouldn't work — various parts of his house were being remodeled so it was a mess. Then when those projects were done, he had relatives staying. On and on. I even wondered if he was married or had a girlfriend since he was so adept at keeping me out of his place. But he was so loving and attentive I pushed that thought aside.

I noticed he had a reason to decline attending every social event to which I invited him. So he never met my friends. I told him it was important to me that we were in each other's social lives. But he never invited me to meet his friends, so it felt like he was keeping me at arms length the whole time.

He declined attending every social event to which I invited him

When he visited, he'd take me out to dinner or to the movies. But our physical pull was so strong, before or after — or often both — we'd end up you know where. I tried not to think that this was a purely sexual relationship because he was attentive in between trysts. But the absence of any social interaction with the other's friends eventually made it clear that he didn't want a real relationship with me.

Finally, after telling me many times how perfect we were for each other, how much I meant to him, and how he envisioned being with me for decades, he declared we weren't compatible. I suppose the chemistry ran its course for him. I was heartbroken, even though I could see we had major differences in our relationship goals, preferences and expectations. Still, it stings to have someone you are attracted to break up with you, even if your logical self knows it isn't going to work.

The lesson — which I could have told myself beforehand if I were advising someone else — is to take it slow. Make sure you both truly want the same thing. Even if you both say you want an exclusive, committed long-term relationship, you don't really know what that exactly means to the other until you've gotten to know each other for a while.

Do I regret this relationship? No. In many ways he taught me important lessons and I will cherish the good times we had together. There were indications of our incompatibility in the second date that I chose to ignore, even when they were repeated. There was so much that I thought worked that I was willing to compromise or chalk up to no relationship being perfect.

Swapping sexual favors for...dog sitting!

A former flame recently told me an old girlfriend, who ended their relationship extremely badly, asked if he'd take care of her dogs while she's on vacation. When he said yes, but wouldn't accept any money for it, she offered to give him sexual services in exchange for dog sitting. She'd even designed a sexual-favors credit system where he earned rolls in the hay for strolls with the dogs. He was flabbergasted!

Although when they broke up 10 months ago she wrote him a letter listing his every flaw — and insulting his masculinity — evidentially his in-the-sack performance was now missed. And while she wasn't suggesting they get back in relationship, she was more than suggesting they get back in bed.

She offered to give him sexual services in exchange for dog sitting

Is this what's in store for modern-day singles? A new perspective on the f___-buddy concept? The attitude of, "You take care of my dogs and I'll take care of you"? What's next? "Pick up my mail and I'll give you a quick pick me up." "Water my plants and I'll make your mouth water." "You do me this favor and I'll do you a sexual favor." While we admired her creativity designing a credit system, it seemed to us a tad too much like prostitution.

"Sex: A Man's Guide"

I thought this would pique your interest!

But, since mostly women are reading this, why am I writing about men's sex?

When I began to put my toe in the dating water, I realized I had been intimate with only one man in the past 20 years. I wondered what might have changed. What should I be aware of that I didn't need to worry about much with pre-marriage intimacy in the '70s and '80s? For example, I knew virtually nothing about STDs and decided I should educate myself.

What has changed from pre-marriage intimacy in the '70s and '80s?

At my library's book sale *Sex: A Man's Guide* jumped out at me. Nearly literally. A friend shopping with me pulled it from the piles and said I needed it. I flipped through it and agreed. I figured I should know what guys know — or at least should know. I read the 478 pages in one sitting — then had to take a cold shower.

It was so informative I decided to make it my coffee table book. It is quite a conversation piece, with dinner party guests taking turns reading aloud especially provocative parts.

I decided it would be a great test for gentleman callers. I toyed with putting Post-It Notes peeking out from particular pages on how to please a woman. Then I could later see if he had done his homework. I considered leaving the book on the coffee table, putting a hair on the cover before a guy came over, then excusing myself, and later seeing if he'd picked it up. That's an old detective trick — I'd know because the hair would be gone.

Most guys, pals as well as suitors, were interested in it immediately. Some asked why I had it; however, most didn't. But they weren't turning to the parts I wanted them to. They turned to "prostate problems," "erectile dysfunction," and "male G-spot." Drat! My plan did not go as I imagined.

Still, it is a good read. Just make sure you have time for a cold shower afterward.

What is sexy?

"Sex appeal is 50% what you've got and 50% what people think you've got." —Sophia Loren

What is sexiness? To me it is a confidence, a strong sense of self, not arrogance. It doesn't have to do with body size or shape or facial beauty. I've known people who were sexy but not particularly physically attractive. A friend of mine is a burn victim, having scars over most of his body, including his face. Yet he is a babe magnet. I rarely see him without a beautiful woman — or several — surrounding him. He's been married three times.

Do you think you are sexy? If so, do you allow it to show? Do you wear clothes that show off the best parts of your body without looking slutty? Do you smile, flirt and play with men? Does your walk show confidence? Do you put your best foot forward in public? These all contribute to that mysterious "sexiness."

Do you smile, flirt and play with men?

What do you think is sexy in men? I am partial to easy smiles, long-sleeved shirts with the sleeves rolled up, a great fitting suit with an impeccably tied tie (small knot), goatees, good posture, a tuft of chest hair peeking out of an open-collared neckline, intelligence, humor, kindness, strong biceps and chivalry. I once went out with a man because a pic in his profile showed him with a great smile and biceps the size of my thighs. (OK, nothing is as big as my thighs, but you get the picture. Unfortunately, the in-person version was not as enticing as the picture.)

Describe what you think is sexy. This is not all the attributes of your perfect mate, but what you find sexy. If it is personified in Richard Gere, Taye Diggs, Sean Connery, Johnny Depp, Colin Farrell or Tom Cruise, what is it that makes them sexy to you? When you articulate it clearly, it will be easier to spot. Don't cop out with "I know it when I see it."

Men and women see sex differently

I am continually flummoxed by how men and women seem to see sex so totally differently. From my experience, it seems that men take sex much less seriously than women. I know I'm generalizing here. There are always exceptions, but stay with me.

It dawned on me that the difference is similar to that old joke about the chicken and the pig looking at the breakfast sign in the window. It said "ham and egg breakfast." The pig turned to the chicken and said "For you, it's just a contribution. For me it's total commitment."

Many women, although not all, see having sex as a sign that there is a commitment to the relationship. Men, although I realize not all, seem to be more cavalier. Sex, it seems, is considered merely a very enjoyable physical release. And to do it with another, even someone they're not particularly drawn to, makes the experience significantly better. With someone they are attracted to, it is one of the best experiences on the planet. But, if the man is immature or less evolved, he doesn't seem to appreciate that the woman can have a very different relationship with sex.

Often a man will press toward doing the deed without exploring what it would mean to the woman. He may not ask her philosophy on sex, and if they do it, whether they have similar expectations about behaviors afterward. Would they spend the night together, rather than one getting up and going home? Would she expect to talk every day and see each other regularly? Does it mean exclusivity? What, exactly, would he be getting himself into, other than her pants? Would he be opening himself up to constant phone calls, tirades when he doesn't call, even visits to work or other unpleasant behaviors, just because of a little roll in the hay?

What would he be getting himself into, other than her pants?

A lot of tension, strife, and upset could be avoided if there was an adult conversation about sex — not only the physical issue of protection, but the emotional expectations, implications and ramifications as well. If both had their rational wits about them before they plunged forward with their physical cravings, it would prevent a lot of angst on one or both parts.

So why isn't this conversation common, since it makes so much sense? My theory is that passion can

evolve rather quickly, and one thing can definitely lead quickly to another. And soon you are further along than you would have rationally decided to be. But it feels so good you don't think (much) about stopping. Your animalistic urges trump your sensible, prudent, mature sound mind.

The only way I can see to avoid this is to have the conversation when you aren't in the middle of a passionate embrace. I know, sometimes you don't know that you're going to be in a passionate embrace until it's happening. But if you have the presence of mind to call a "time out" and discuss it, you can always pick up where you left off. What if he gets upset that you stopped the action to have this discussion? Then it's great that you know that now so you can release him back into the dating pool. He really isn't interested in having more than a booty call with you.

Be clear on what sex means to you. Do you care if he sleeps with others while sleeping with you? Do you think it's OK for you to sleep with others concurrently? Do you expect you'll both be exclusive? Do you think it means you're now in a relationship and you will talk to and see each other regularly? Does it mean spending the whole night together, not going home right afterward? The clearer you are, the easier this conversation will be.

Getting naked with him the first time

Many midlife singles haven't been intimate with someone other than their long-term mate for a long time. A common concern is that your body is not the same as it was when you were younger. You have what Bridget Jones called "wobbly bits." So the prospect of getting undressed with someone is unnerving. So much so, that it may prevent you from putting your toe in the dating pool.

The prospect of getting undressed with someone is unnerving

Hopefully, you don't choose to become intimate with someone until you have dated him for a while. At that point, it is really a moot point because he will have seen you in different attire so knows your body's pros and cons and will love you for you, and not focus on your less-than-perfect body parts. As one male pal put it, "When you're naked we know we're going to get sex, so we don't focus on any imperfection. We're just very happy!"

My first post-marriage naked experience was with a man I'd been dating for a while. He was 100 pounds overweight so I had little concern he'd judge my larger-than-normal bumps and curves. I was right. In fact, I learned that some men love women who are, as one friend put it, "umpa lumpa."

If a man criticizes you when you are unclothed, that is a good sign he is not the right man for you. Even if you are not happy with your body, he should have the good sense to shut up, even if you are complaining about your stretch marks, cellulite, chubby thighs, etc.

Dating sex questions from a midlife dating freshman

My neighbor is just starting dating after a 30-year absence. Two weeks ago she joined a service that matches her and men with comparable intellect, education, income and personality. She's had dates with three men. She had questions for me — many questions!

Frosh: You have been dating a lot longer than I have. I'm a freshman and you're a senior. Tell me the rules.

DG: There really are no rules. You decide what works for you. You make the rules.

Frosh: There have to be rules.

DG: There is the book, *The Rules*.

Frosh: Yes, but it doesn't cover what I need. I want to know other rules.

DG: About what?

Frosh: Should you kiss on the first date?

DG: Kiss if you want to. If you don't, and he's coming in for a lip lock, turn your head so he busses your cheek. When I hear myself think, 'I want to kiss him,' it's a good sign. Sometimes I get kissed by guys without my thinking this, and it can still be good. But it's better if I know I want to kiss him.

Frosh: When do you have sex?

DG: When it feels like the right time for both of you.

Frosh: On the first date?

DG: If you want. I don't. In fact, studies show that most men don't consider a woman a long-term relation-ship prospect if they sleep together on the first date, *Few men turn down the opportunity to sleep with a woman if she's willing.* although few turn down the opportunity if she's willing.

Frosh: See, that's a rule!

DG: If you want to make it one. Rule: No first-date sex. Unless you both just want a one-night stand.

Frosh: What if a man wants to progress faster than you do?

DG: You tell him you're not ready. In fact, that's a great phrase I didn't learn for a while: 'I'm not ready to do that.' It works great to slow things down.

Frosh: So what if he wants to go to second or third base and you're not ready?

DG: You tell him so, while removing his hand and putting it where you are comfortable. If he persists, extricate yourself. 'I'm not feeling comfortable so I'm going home.' Or if he's at your place, 'I've enjoyed our time together, but it's time for you to go now.' Be pleasant but firm.

Frosh: I've heard there's a rule for how many dates before you have sex.

DG: There's not really a rule. Some guys have a 3-date rule. If they don't have sex by the third date, they bail. Greg Behrendt said he has a 10-date rule. He thinks people fall into bed too quickly, and they should wait for 10 dates to see if they are compatible enough to have sex. It's different for everyone, but it is good to talk about it early and see what his expectation is. You may not be ready by the third date. That's okay. If he's not willing to wait 'til you're ready, he's not for you.

Frosh: Women all have different sexual satisfaction

needs. Do guys know that?

DG: Some do. Some don't. If he's only been with one woman for 20 or 30 years, he learned, I hope, how to satisfy her. Some think that they will try the same techniques with you and seem flummoxed when they don't create the same results. You need to gently teach him by telling him what you like and ask for what you want. If he doesn't comply or forgets next time, he's not interested in pleasing you enough to pay attention. Not a good sign.

Frosh: So what you're really saying is I get to make up the rules?

DG: Exactly. Women hold the power to progress or not. Yes, a guy can pull the plug at any time, but it is the woman who decides when it is okay to move forward. So you need to be present to what you want and how you're feeling.

Frosh: That's a rule I would have never known. I thought the guys had the power. I need to think through what I want, and if something is uncomfortable I need to say something. That is very empowering! Thanks!

DG: You're very welcome. I had to learn all this these past few years, so I am glad to pass on some of what I've gleaned.

Beware the massage seduction

t's happened since high school. But if you've been absent from dating 20 or 30 years, you may have forgotten this maneuver.

Sometimes when a man wants to get closer physically, he'll offer you a shoulder or back massage, or he'll just start kneading your shoulders. If you respond positively, he'll continue.

Watch out for this ploy. This happens so often, I'd swear it is taught in a "how to seduce women" class. So catch on quickly. It is often a way to get you to undress or into bed. Here's how it goes.

Him: You seem tense. Would you like a shoulder massage?

You: I do feel stressed. Yes, thank you. That would be great.

Him: (Massaging your shoulders) Your shoulders do seem tight. I can feel knots.

You: (Closing your eyes) That feels so good. Ummm.

Him: (Working down your back) Good. I can feel knots down here too. Can I unhook your bra to get under the strap?

You: Sure.

Him: (After a few minutes he pulls your top out of your pants and massages your back directly) How's this?

You: Great. You have good hands.

Him: Why don't you lie on the couch (or floor or bed) so I can have better leverage.

You: (Complying) Okay.

Him: (After a few minutes) You know, I could do a better job if I didn't have to wrestle with your blouse. Can you take it off?

You: (Trustingly) Sure.

That's the beginning of the end. Soon he begins kissing your shoulders and back, massaging your butt and legs, then under your pants, then he takes those off too. You're now deeper than you imagined, all

You're now deeper than you imagined, all from naiveté

from the naiveté that a shoulder massage will be just that. Just as the frog got cooked by small increments in the slowly boiling water, you have gotten yourself in hot water by trusting and not saying no to any of the small steps. If you don't say "no" or "stop" along the way, you are allowing yourself to be seduced a bit at a time.

If you want to be seduced, fine. But if you didn't think, "I'd love to make love with Mr. X" you'll find yourself doing more than you'd planned. Just be fore-warned so you know the signs along the way and say "stop" any time you don't want to go forward.

The sex talk

I'm surprised when a man expresses he wants to have sex, but he doesn't then initiate a discussion of protection. I guess there's an assumption condoms will be used, but how much more reassuring it would be if he brings up the issue rather than me. If he were to say, "I would love to make love to you when you're ready, and know that I believe in only protected sex until we both have had recent STD tests." That shows he cares about you as well as himself and is mature about this issue.

Let's say it is clear you both want to have sex. How do you bring up the discussion of protection, STDs and testing? It is not a sexy subject, but if you are able to discuss it maturely, when not in the heat of passion, it shows you are unafraid of uncomfortable conversations.

In my experience, it seems that men are ready sooner than women. The "3-date rule" for sex seems arbitrary. One man I dated for 6 weeks kept saying "I can wait. I'm not going anywhere." Then he broke up with me in an Instant Message. I guess he wasn't going anywhere but his own house, as he never came to mine again!

Ever since a guy revealed he had genital herpes during a first date and we'd scheduled a second, I've taken STDs much more seriously. I researched herpes and discovered that it can be contagious even when the person is not currently having an outbreak. According to herpes medication manufacturer Valtrex, 70% of people got genital herpes from their partner when they were showing no signs of the virus (like an outbreak). According to the Centers for Disease Control and Prevention, 1 out of 5 American teenagers and adults is infected with it.

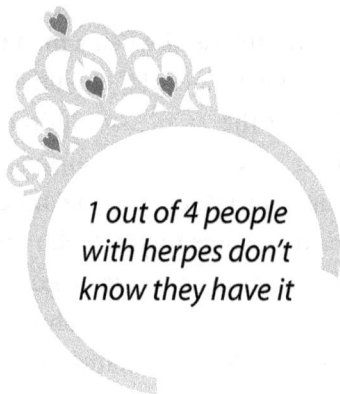

1 out of 4 people with herpes don't know they have it

If your partner says "I'm disease free," how does he know if he hasn't been tested? One source says 1 out of 4 people with herpes don't know they have it and, of course, they can still spread it.

In a recent study, college students were asked to anonymously answer some questions about sex. One of the questions was if they knew they had an STD and they thought they were going to get lucky that night would they tell their partner. An astonishing number (I'm sorry, I wish I had the data) said "no." And the majority of those who said "no" were men. Now we'd hope midlife men would have more maturity and honesty, but it is not a given.

The bottom line: show each other the test results before doing anything that could spread a disease. If there has been sex with someone else after the test was taken, get tested now, then wait for the results before moving forward. If he balks, you know he doesn't care about your safety and peace of mind, so he's not the one for you. He's cavalier about something that can not only affect your health, but in the case of AIDS, can take your life.

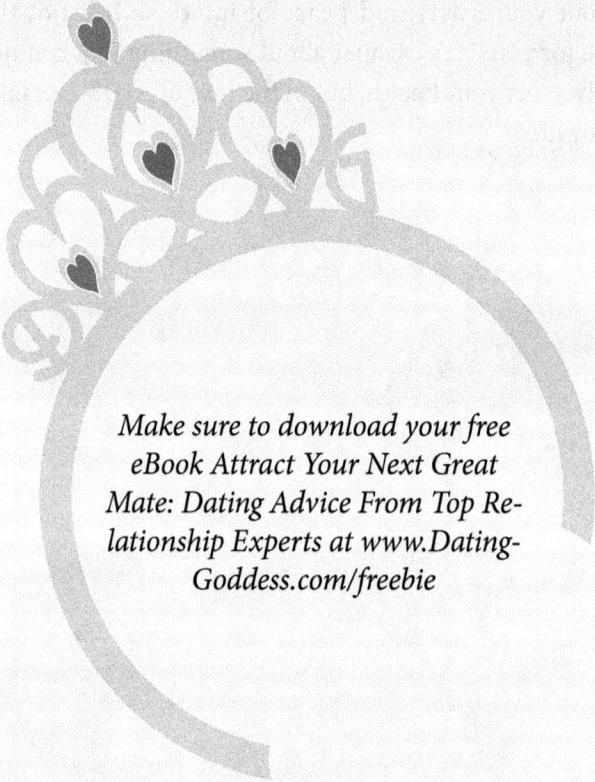

Make sure to download your free eBook Attract Your Next Great Mate: Dating Advice From Top Relationship Experts at www.Dating-Goddess.com/freebie

An excuse to seduce or how important is bedroom bliss?

Really the question is, how important is finding out if you're sexual compatible early in a relationship?

A pal told me his sister began dating a man. She told her guy she'd decided to wait six months before having sex because in the past she'd fallen into bed with men too early and then the relationship didn't work out. She wanted to make sure that her next relationship was on solid ground before making love. Waiting six months would ensure they had a strong foundation.

Waiting six months would ensure they had a strong foundation

33

When the six-month mark approached, they arranged a romantic weekend getaway. The scene was set. They were both giddy with anticipation. However, after the big event, she was disappointed. They didn't click between the sheets. She told her brother she had to break up with her beau, as he didn't do it for her.

Another woman shared she'd broken up with her boyfriend because he didn't satisfy her in the bedroom. She tried to explain what she liked, but he either didn't listen or didn't comply.

So my guy pal has decided it's important to find out if there is bedroom bliss soon in the relationship. If not, he feels it's best to move on. I don't know if this is just his excuse to seduce a woman early on, but the way he explained it, it made perfect sense.

After a 20+-year "unsatisfying" marriage, a divorced woman friend says it's important to find out if a new guy's able to give her horizontal happiness before investing too much time in him.

However, what all these folks are missing, I think, is that sexual compatibility can take some time creating. Everyone has a different idea of what floats their boat, and feeling comfortable explaining that takes trust. And trust often takes time.

Bottom line: If it isn't great the first time, talk about what you want and try a few more times. If it isn't happening for you then, there's a breakdown that may not be able to be fixed.

Would you lie to get laid?

The Dentyne "Happy Hunting" guide is designed to help young men and women seem more attractive to each other. For example, it gives some fake stories you can use to impress the other sex (e.g., you were in a commercial as a kid, backup dancer in a rap video, won a big payout in a slot machine).

It has "business cards with attitude" templates that allow you to fill in your name and number and a printable PDF will be downloaded. Women could pose as a belly dance instructor, runway model, beer quality control, sex therapist, or lingerie designer. Men can pretend to be a game developer, poker instructor, pilot or movie location coordinator.

There are printable photos of your supposed hot car, lake house, dog, race horse, motorcycle, etc., to have in your wallet to show your potential date.

It will tutor you so you can assume an accent (French, Italian and British for men; French, Italian and

Swedish for women). Guys can choose customizable clippings of them supposedly doing something heroic. And women get tutoring in "guy talk" about sports, financial info, and male movies.

So the message is you aren't good enough to make someone interested in you based on who you are. You have to pretend to be someone more accomplished, interesting, or foreign. I thought society had progressed to the point where it was perfectly fine to be honestly and unabashedly who you are, and if someone doesn't find you compelling, then just move on.

While the Dentyne campaign is amusing, what messages does it send to singles — especially young singles? They have to lie to get a date? This is the wrong message. If you don't think you're very interesting, go out and do something to make yourself more so.

Do you need your sexual pilot light lit?

In an interview with Gail Sheehy about her book *Sex & The Seasoned Woman* she talks about having "a pilot-light lover — a transitional figure who comes into a midlife woman's life and reawakens her excitement about sex and love. He usually doesn't last. He's not a keeper, but she has to celebrate his role in her life because he makes her feel womanly again. Then she's ready for the next phase."

Mine was not a pilot-light *lover*, but someone who reminded me that I was still sexy and desirable. Four months after my ex left I was still reeling from the pain of feeling discarded. I'd thought we had a loving, passionate relationship, so his leaving left me doubting my view of the world and myself.

At a party with colleagues, in walked a tall drink of water. Good looking and athletic, he was a new face. I was drawn to him immediately. As luck would have it, he took the chair next to me so we began to chat.

He was smart, funny, and seemed focused only on

me. He knew of me, although I didn't know him, so he discussed my work and accomplishments. I was flattered to get this much attention from such a good-looking, charming guy. We openly flirted. The conversations and images of those around us faded until it felt that it was just the two of us in the room.

After a while, all the guests crowded into the living room to sing "Happy Birthday." I made a short detour so when I arrived no seats were left. He motioned for me to share his chair. It felt so wonderful to be so close to a sexy, attentive man that I didn't want to get up even though it was extremely uncomfortable balancing on a small chair with him.

We talked for hours. By the end of the day I was enamored. His long, delicious good-bye hug made me sure he'd call me within 24 hours. He didn't. When he did call, he asked me for some business advice. I saw that he was not interested in me romantically, but only as a business pal. I'd deluded myself that this 10-year-younger man was a potential beau. Now we are good friends and continue our flirting, as well as sharing dating stories.

I am grateful for him rekindling a passion that I'd let hibernate after my marriage broke up. As I got to know him, I saw we wouldn't make a good couple. But fantasizing about him helped ignite my pilot light.

The sexual audition

Some people feel it is important to discover if you are sexually compatible before spending time developing a relationship with someone. Others feel that sex is something that should happen after a firm foundation of trust and caring has been developed.

If you are in the first camp, then your first time having sex together is a sort of audition. You, and perhaps your partner, are assessing if the other is a good lover, sexually generous and satisfying. What is the proof? There is generally only one way you (or he) determines if there is a match: if whomever is making the determination is satisfied, although some include the other's satisfaction as part of the criteria.

Your first time having sex together is a sort of audition

The rub is that if one of you has a challenge that prevents you from achieving satisfaction, the other is often blamed. Certain medications can impair one's libido and performance. A man who has ED or can't be satisfied blames the woman. If he experiences this more than a time or two, he ends the relationship. He will either become obnoxious to make the woman break up with him, or he'll walk away, making up lame excuses.

Perhaps he is embarrassed that he can't perform. Or it takes him a long time. Or he has to start over several times. Or nothing he does seems to excite you. Or it's not enough.

It can be frustrating because you have been drawn enough to each other to want to get closer sexually. If you both are willing to work on it, to talk about it without blame or embarrassment, sometimes the situation can be changed. But if this is a part of a romantic relationship that is important to you, unless something shifts, perhaps it's best to admit that the audition is a failure and move on.

"Would you like the recipe for how to seduce me?"

"You know that 'look' women get when they want sex? Me neither." –Steve Martin

You've been dating a special guy for a while. You feel connected and closer to him than you've felt about others. He says and shows that he feels similarly. You want to take your relationship to the next level.

Most couples stumble into intimacy. It happens pretty haphazardly, and a great deal depends on how you're feeling at the moment. If you are both feeling it, one thing leads to the proverbial other, and soon you are hurtling along like a speeding train, unable — unwilling, really — to stop.

Sometimes everything seems to work perfectly. But more often, there is some herky-jerkiness, some awkwardness, some "I wish he would…," or "I wonder if he likes…." One of the hardest parts of new intimacy is learning what the other likes — and doesn't like. Most people do whatever worked in their last long-term relationship. For midlife daters that may have been a while ago and they are rusty. And of course, what worked for her may not work for you. If he's savvy, he knows that everyone has their own combination of boat-floaters. You have to learn each others' toe-curling moves.

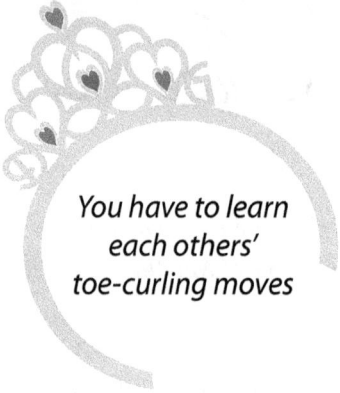

You have to learn each others' toe-curling moves

So how do you get him to learn your seduction secrets? You can see if he picks up on your subtle cues. You can give him positive reinforcement when he does what you like. You can wait for him to ask what gives you ecstasy. However, none of these are the bullet train to Blissville. No jet to Joy City. No rocket to Rapturetown.

Or you can be direct. When you sense he wants to progress and you want him to make some specific moves that get you in the mood, what's to prevent you from saying, "Would you like the recipe for how to seduce me?" I think most men would love a guide for what works with you, rather than trying to figure it out by trial and error.

(Be sure to use language he relates to. If your man cooks, then "recipe" may be the right metaphor. If he likes to build, them perhaps "blueprint" is better. If he's an engineer, then "schematic." A medical professional might respond to "prescription," and a mathematician or chemist might like "formula.")

I'm not suggesting you write out your recipe, although one man sent me an erotic story that described what he liked. Try a verbal description, encouraging him to follow along as you describe it. Professional trainers know that the best learning happens when the learner follows instructions as they are given. ☺

If you were to write up your recipe for how to seduce you, how would it go? For practice, write it out. If your man wants to see it, great, but it will be more fun if you describe it as he puts your instructions into action!

What to ask yourself before getting naked with him

You're really attracted to the guy you've been dating. Things have been heating up and you feel soon you'll be salsa-ing under the sheets. You think he's attractive — perhaps even hot — and you can't keep your hands off each other.

You feel soon you'll be salsa-ing under the sheets

My friend George says he asked himself two questions when dating before deciding to jump into bed with a woman. You may have other questions, but I think these two are a great start. At least they've worked for me.

1. *In the morning, would I look at my date and think this was a good idea?*

   If you project yourself into the future and imagine yourself looking at him next to you in bed, how would you feel? That this was a good idea — or a stupid one? If you envision that you'd feel positive about waking up next to him, tousled hair, morning breath and all, then that is a good sign. However, if you can't conceive spending the whole night next to him, nor waking up to his unshaven mug, perhaps it's best to wait. Of course, if one-night stands are fine for you, then you needn't even ask this question.

2. *How would I feel introducing my date to my friends?*

   Often our friends are more important to us than our dates — until we've fallen head over heels. I've taken some suitors to social events, and later my friends told me, "I just didn't see you two together long term," or "He didn't seem right for you." If you value your friends' insights and assessments, then

   Are you just after a physical release?

you often know whether you would feel proud to introduce your date to them or not. If you don't see introducing your date to your best pals, perhaps it's not a good idea to get naked. Unless, of course, you see this as a one-time occurrence.

If you decide to move forward even after answering "no" to these two questions, ask yourself why. Are you just after a physical release? If you are okay with no-strings-attached sex, what if he sees this as a sign you are more committed to the relationship? Are you leading him on? Is that fair to him? What if you get more emotionally attached after the roll in the hay, yet know you don't think of him as a long-term boyfriend? How will you handle that?

In the heat of passion, often you aren't thinking with your brain. It would head off some heartbreak if you could collect yourself for a few minutes and ask yourself some questions before you decide to move forward. These two questions are a start. Write them in your PDA, or on a paper in your wallet and add your own if you want.

What other questions would you like to ask yourself before deciding to take the relationship forward physically?

Are you and your guy on the same sexual time line?

A male pal and I were discussing how sometimes a dating man and woman's sexual time lines are different. In other words, one is ready to move forward physically before the other.

For the sake of this illustration, we'll assume the man wants things to move more quickly than the woman, although we know the opposite can be true.

My pal explained it like this:

When a man decides he wants to have sex with a woman he's dating, she isn't always ready when he is to take their relationship to that level. It's like sand in an hour glass. When the sand runs out, he feels they had better be in bed, or he leaves the relationship looking for someone who is more in alignment with his time frame.

However, if she isn't ready, she can make the sand slow down by doing some little, but important actions. Some of them include:

- 💜 She can tell him she is attracted to him and can see them being sexual, but she isn't ready yet.

- 💜 She can touch him in non-teasing ways, such as holding hands, hugging, and touching him lovingly.

- 💜 She can kiss and caress him as long as she doesn't send mixed signals and cross any boundaries that she has expressed.

If the above are missing, he thinks she isn't interested or loses patience and the sand runs out quickly.

Have you experienced different sexual time frames with someone you were dating? If you were the one who wasn't ready, how did you still show him you were interested? And if you were ready first, what did he do that showed you he was still interested but not quite yet?

Sharing your sexual owner's manual with him

Have you ever driven a car that seems very foreign to you? I remember driving a friend's Italian sports car that had five gears when I was used to four. The dashboard had a unfamiliar layout. And everything was labeled in Italian!

Or maybe you're a Mac gal and every once in a great while you have to work on a PC (or a PC gal working on a Mac). You know the results you want to create, but you have to really focus to figure out how to open the applications you want. And the keyboard has a different layout than you're used to. While you know you can achieve what you want, it just takes a little longer as the keys and shortcuts you're used to aren't easily apparent.

So it is when becoming intimate with a new guy for the first time in midlife, after you've been with your former mates for years.

You know what you want to accomplish — or what you want him to accomplish. But just like the above examples, the key behaviors he's used to doing — and getting a reasonably predictable response — may not work at all with you. You are an Italian sports car, and he's driven an automatic Chevy truck for 20 years. He's used to turning the key, and the engine hums. Now he tries the same action, but he's forgotten to engage the clutch, so the engine doesn't respond.

Unlike a Mac/ PC, there's not a handy "Help" menu

How do you help your guy have a quick lesson on what makes your motor purr, without insulting him? Unlike the Mac/PC example, there's not a handy "Help" menu he can refer to when flummoxed.

I'm afraid that Help menu or owner's manual is you. And while some men are embarrassed or feel uneasy when you guide him through what works for you, the savvy ones are appreciative. If he wants to make you happy — and why would you be in this position with him if you didn't think he was interested in making you happy? — he will listen and follow instructions. And assuming his efforts are successful, he'll make mental notes for the next time.

And the same goes in reverse. Don't be afraid to ask him what he likes. If he doesn't give you the verbal or nonverbal feedback you're expecting, ask him to share what works. Some men don't like to talk during the act, and if your guy is the silent type, talk about what he likes before the next time. It may seem a bit stilted at first, but you will both have a more satisfying experience. And talking about it ahead of time sometimes heats things up a bit.

And just like with the computer example, you'll want to make sure virus protection is installed.

Having a SNORgasbord with your sweetie

Y ou've been dating the same guy for a while. You've decided it is time to have a sleepover. You follow the rules set forth in "Sleepover do's and don'ts" (page 1).

You're snuggled in his arms, loving the closeness. You begin to drift to slumberland until … he starts snoring in your ear. And not just a sweet little muffled snorting or grunting. But a full-bore snore — the sound of a freight train running through your bedroom, or a foghorn warning the ships to stay at bay — even though you live in Kansas. Maybe he has sleep apnea, which can not only be dangerous, but Mac-truck loud as he begins to breathe again after a temporary cessation.

Two of my beaus had such deafening snoring I slept on the couch in other parts of the house to get away from the cacophonous noise. Even with ear plugs,

I could still hear them! Once at a hotel, there was no-where to escape. I was a hair's breadth away from drag-ging a blanket and pillow to the walk-in closet to sleep — until I realized it was only 20-feet away and wouldn't make much difference.

Maybe you're the snorter, emitting a short guttural sound with each breath. Or perhaps your sound is like a very large — and loud — gaggle of geese honking overhead.

If only one of you snores, it can cause unrest

If only one of you snores, it can cause un-rest (bad pun, I know). How can you have a snugglefest with your sweetie if you can't sleep in the same room? Do you develop a routine of cuddling then retreat to the guest room or couch for sleep?

If both of you snore, however, it is a snorgasbord! As long as one of you doesn't awaken the other with your nocturnal racket, you can both enjoy snuggling while snoring.

According to Breathe Right, "Snoring affects 50 mil-lion — more than half — of all U.S. households." They make the newest version of what I consider a "marital aid." No, not the kind that has been around for decades. I'm talking about nasal strips.

I've asked snoring sleep partners to use these and

they nearly always significantly reduced the frequency and volume of the braying. I consider them relationship life savers, along with comfortable ear plugs and breath mints.

Breathe Right even has a Snore-O-Meter that let's you listen to four kinds of snorers. Great! Like I haven't heard enough snoring to last a lifetime?

Have you stayed just because of the sex?

When midlife daters have shared about their unfulfilling multi-month or -year relationships, I've asked why they stayed. After complaining about their former sweetie's selfishness, immaturity, miserliness, controlling, and/or downright meanness it seems to me you'd be a fool to stay in this relationship. I'm astonished when I hear a commonly cited reason for staying: "The sex was good."

What is this hold that good sex has over many people that they will stay in a bad relationship just because of it? Are they so fearful they won't find a good mate and good sex that they languish with someone who's not a good fit because of this scarcity mentality?

Before online dating, many midlife daters report it was difficult to meet someone to go out with. After the usual sources of friends, work, church, gym, classes, singles events and the grocery store produce section, there was not a steady stream of potential mates to be found. So it seems people would cling to whomever met at least a minimum standard. And for some that minimum standard was good sex.

Both men and women have told me they want to be in the sack with someone early on to see if there is sexual compatibility. (See "An excuse to seduce," page 33) While I think this is important, I believe it is more important to have overall compatibility. As I shared in "Would you like the recipe to seduce me" (page 41) and "Sharing your sexual owner's manual with him" (page 51), "good sex" is something that is different for everyone so, to some degree, must be learned.

So why would you stay with someone just because of something that can be learned — and taught — assuming your partner has an interest in learning as well as teaching? To me it would be like staying with someone who is a good cook. While it's great to have someone who already knows how to cook your favorite dishes, if he doesn't but is really interested in learning, most can learn what will please you.

I better understand why people have an eight- or ten-date, or 3-month sex rule. It helps you know if you are really a good fit before making the plunge. And it will prevent you staying with someone who isn't a good match just because of the sex.

Have you stayed in a not-great relationship just because of good sex?

Why do midlife daters have sex?

You might have heard of the study released from University of Texas at Austin psychology researchers David Buss, Ph.D. and Cindy Meston, Ph.D. on why human beings have sex.

However, upon closer examination, I see that the study was based mostly on undergraduate students (1500 of the 1900 subjects were students; approx. 400 were from a separate study of men and women aged 17-52). It doesn't take a genius to deduce that college students have sex for reasons that, hopefully, don't exactly parallel people over 50. Only a PR person would universalize the results into the headline of the release, "Why Do People Have Sex?"

The Texas psychologists identified four major factors and 13 sub-factors for why people (e.g., college students) have sex:

♥ Physical reasons such as to reduce stress ("It seemed like good exercise"), feel pleasure ("It's

exciting"), improve or expand experiences
("I was curious about sex"), and the physical
desirability of their partner ("The person was
a good dancer"). While we could agree with
"It's exciting," are midlife daters comparably
curious about sex? I doubt it. And I doubt they
commonly have sex with someone because of
their partner's
dancing prow-
ess. Possibly, but
probably not
frequently; oth-
erwise midlife
men and
women would
be stampeding
Arthur Murray
dance studios.
"It seemed like
good exercise"? Please. This reasoning is for
those who hate to pump iron, but think they
can boff to get buff.

*Think they can
boff to get buff*

💜 Goal-based reasons, including utilitarian or
practical considerations ("I wanted to have a
baby"), social status ("I wanted to be popu-
lar") and revenge ("I wanted to give someone
else a sexually transmitted disease"). All of
these examples are immature. Hopefully no
reasonably intelligent and psychologically
sound midlifer would consider these adequate
reasons. If you are sane and mature, you know

that getting pregnant with someone you don't desire to be with long-term or haven't discussed their co-parenting, is asking for a heap of hurt. And while I know that sex has brought people social status by sleeping with someone in a higher social strata so they can assume that person's lifestyle, it is often short lived. And anyone who purposefully transmits an STD should have the parts involved with this transfer removed. Without anesthesia.

💚 Emotional reasons such as love and commitment ("I wanted to feel connected") and expression ("I wanted to say 'thank you'"). Emotional reasons, yes. I wanted to say "thank you"? Send a card!

💚 Insecurity-based reasons, including self-esteem ("I wanted the attention"), a feeling of duty or pressure ("My partner kept insisting") and to guard a mate ("I wanted to keep my partner from straying"). Yes, even midlife daters can suffer from self-esteem issues. Yes, some have sex for the same reason as these college students: "I wanted the attention." Or perhaps "I was afraid if I didn't have sex with him he'd stop calling." Same with duty or pressure: "We'd reached the third (or some arbitrary number) date and I knew he expected it, or had 'earned' it." And yes, to try to secure someone's loyalty seems a reason without age limits.

Why do you think midlife daters have sex? Which of the above reasons correspond to midlifers and which reasons are different for us?

What women need from a man before having sex

Laws of the Jungle: Dating for Women Over 40 co-authors Gloria MacDonald and Thelma Beam interviewed midlife women and asked how they knew they wanted to have sex with a specific man. Filtering through the answers, they came up with some commonalities for the women's description of chemistry, a term that seems elusive.

The components of chemistry for women boiled down to four things:

1. Liking and respecting the man; his self-confidence and presentation; kindness, generosity, protectiveness, chivalry and other positive traits; personal acceptability in terms of status, income, personality, etc.

2. The possibility that the relationship will

continue; that some potential exists to make it permanent; that this man could be a suitable life partner for them and they can visualize what their future would be like.

3. The man is willing to invest in her emotionally and materially, shown by cuddling, talking, kindness, acts of service, love talk, generally taking an interest in things that make her happy, gift-giving, paying for outings, having an adequate income. She could envision him willing to commit to a monogamous relationship; that his affections are not otherwise engaged by a former wife/girlfriend or current love interest.

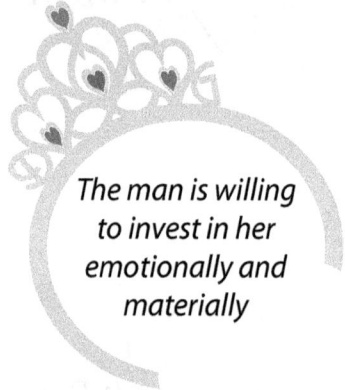

The man is willing to invest in her emotionally and materially

4. That there is at least some physical attraction on both side, or at least that there are no physical turn-offs.

Contrast that with what they learned from single midlife men about what they need to have sex with a woman:

1. He finds her physically attractive.

2. She is willing.

Women report that without many or all of the four criteria, sex is unfulfilling and pointless.

But you can see that women and men approach sex from different places. Only after having sex with a woman will many men decide whether to further invest in the relationship. They will expend time, energy, attention and money to get sex, and women misinterpret this as an investment in the relationship. Men would start a relationship with sex; for women sex is the point at which many other criteria have been met.

Before any male bashing and name calling, hold on. MacDonald and Beam explain the differences logically based on human evolution, and it makes sense. From back to cave people's time, women are wired to want to make sure a man will stick around if she has his children. And men are wired that this isn't that important. Yes, modern men and women have evolved socially, intellectually, and emotionally. Yet, the authors argue, there are still some remnants of that old thinking that is just hard wired for both sexes.

What do you think of their findings? Do you agree with the four criteria they listed? Or do you have different criteria?

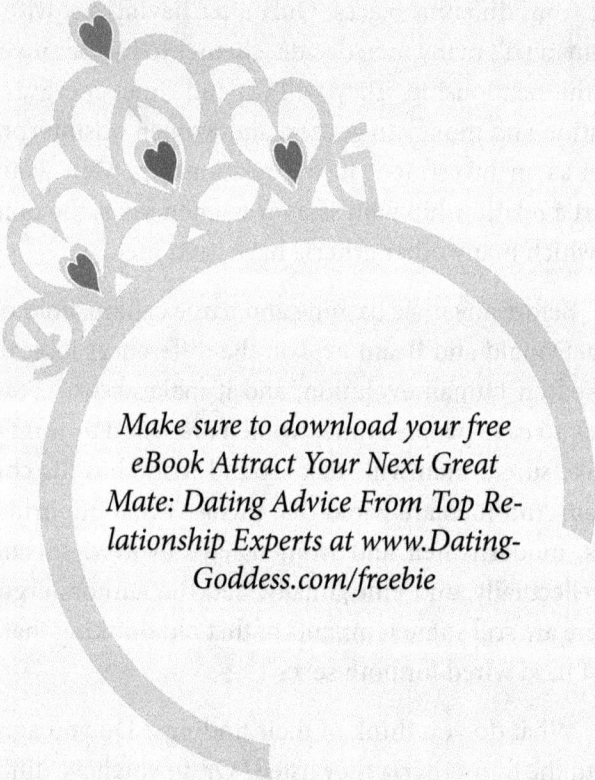

Make sure to download your free
eBook *Attract Your Next Great
Mate: Dating Advice From Top Relationship Experts* at www.Dating-
Goddess.com/freebie

Why too-soon midlife sex is like non-fat food

A guy I started seeing a week ago and I were discussing the lessons we've learned about jumping in the sack too soon. I shared what I reported in "What women need from a man before having sex" (page 65) — that women need to have an emotional connection to make the physical part satisfying. He asked why I didn't think sex with a guy I've known just a week wasn't satisfying. (He was teasing me, since we'd only been seeing each other a week.) I said:

💜 It's all just physical at that point, so early in the relationship. You don't really know each other. I know, you're saying, "What's wrong with that?" It's mechanical. While it can feel nice, it isn't nearly as fantastic as when there's an emotional connection. When you know what it feels like with the latter, the former just isn't really worth it.

💜 It's like non-fat milk after you've had whole milk. Or soy bacon after pork bacon. Or non-fat food after the real thing. Or imitation anything. You know what the real stuff feels/ tastes like, and the other is just too far off to really make it worth it. If you have to partake in the fake stuff (because you're on a diet, the real stuff isn't available, or you have digestion problems), then you learn to tolerate — and in some situations even like — the substitute. But when you have no restrictions, you will only go for the real thing.

While I know there are exceptions when you've felt fantastically close to a guy within a few hours or dates, generally it takes a while to create a bond. And for some, albeit few, women that connection isn't necessary. But from Adventures in Delicious Dating After 40 readers' reports as well as the studies I've read, sex too soon is commonly unsatisfying for most midlife women. Even if you think you're connected before going down that road — to the bedroom — you often exit the hay-rolling highway not feeling entirely happy. Something was missing.

You often exit the hay-rolling highway not feeling entirely happy

One of the great things about midlife dating is you have more lessons from your history that inform your current decisions. You know how you felt in the past when something didn't turn out like you wanted. You can now more easily delay gratification — at least presumed gratification — because you know what needs to be in place for you to feel the way you want. You can control your urges (at least let's hope you can) much better than when you were younger. You have different motivations and can apply your hard-won wisdom to your behaviors.

In other words, you can wait until you have what you need before progressing. There's no need to jump into bed just because you are hot for each other. You know there are other considerations beyond physical, sexual attraction. You are wiser and can dial back your animalistic desires for the benefit of longer-term payoffs.

What are the lessons you've learned about midlife sex before there's been an emotional connection? What are the signs of that connection for you?

Sexual desire is alive and well in daters over 50

A pal sent a link to the article, "Sex, Lust And Passion Top Baby Boomer Love Expectations" to mull over. According to a study conducted by Wanobe.com, "The Lifestyle Place for Those Over Fifty," a UK site, singles over 50 are twice as likely as their younger counterparts to have sex on the first date. I wonder how this would compare to how Yanks would respond. Are Americans looser and hornier than our UK brethren, or more reserved because of our country's Puritan forebears?

They surveyed more than a thousand 50- to 65-year-olds who were members of Europe's largest dating service. Thirty-seven percent of the over 50's said they'd have sex on a first date compared to 18% of the under 40's. (So what happens if you're between 40 and 50?) Are the midlifers more sexually liberal because we grew up during the sexual revolution? Or are we more comfortable with the notion of casual sex? The latter seems counter to what I've read about Boomers and dating sex, which is that midlifers aren't as run by their hormones, and they are willing to wait for sex until they have a strong tie with the person they have been seeing.

The survey's wording is interesting. It asked, "Would you have sex on the first date?" "Would" is different than "have." Lots of horny people would have sex any time — but they don't have the opportunity. So given the chance to have sex on a date with someone who has agreed to spend the evening with you — hey, sure!

The report doesn't break down the data by male/female. So let's guess at the numbers. If the respondents were evenly divided, and 72% of the men said yes, only 2% of the women would have to say yes to make the total 37%. Even if we double the women's percentage to 4%, it means

Most women still have some stigma around doing the deed on the first date

70% of the men would say yes. This seems about right, based on what my readers have shared and I've gleaned from other sources. Not that women aren't as horny as men — but I think most women still have some stigma around doing the deed on the first date. I would be very surprised if a nearly equal number of women and men responded yes.

Interestingly, 76% of the women who said they'd have sex on the first date said they wanted to be "wooed" by their date first, and they expected the man to pick

up the bill. So if he buys dinner, you'll have sex, but if he doesn't, no? And I thought buying sex from non-sex workers was dead! So the truth is the women respondents just didn't want to be a cheap date! I wonder if fish and chips qualifies as "wooing."

Just for fun, let's say the 37% is equally divided between men and women. So 370 total said they'd have sex on the first date, 185 men, 185 women. Seventy-six percent (women wanting to be wooed first) equals 141 women. So a bit more than a quarter of all the women respondents (28%) say they'd like the man to buy them dinner first. That feels like a reasonable percentage.

And those surveyed don't just want sex — they want it NOW! Seventy-three percent of respondents "intend to find a fulfilling sexual relationship in the next 12 months, while 84% want a full sexual relationship with the next person they meet." Read that again — "the next person they meet." What if you are the lucky recipient of an email from that person and you accept an invitation for a drink. Do you think that person may be a tad sexually overwrought? A bit sexually aggressive? Have different expectations for the encounter than you might have? This certainly explains a lot of the inappropriate first-date behavior we've discussed in the Adventures in Delicious Dating After 40 books.

The good news is this study shows that midlifers are still interested in being sexual and passionate — at least those answering the survey, which was pitched to members of a dating site, which makes sense, doesn't it? If someone wasn't interested in romance and passion, s/

he wouldn't be likely to join a dating site, right? So the study is skewed because of the self-selection.

What do you think about this study? Does it seem right to you, or are Americans a different breed? How would you answer if you were asked the question, "Would you have sex on a first date?"

Looking for a connection

"I've had a lot of sex in my life. I'm looking for a connection. Sex is an important element in a long-term relationship, but it's not the only important thing." My jaw was agape as I heard my date share his philosophy.

I admit it. I've come to expect the polar opposite from midlife men in the dating scene. Not that they can't be great guys. But — at least in my 3.5 years of dating — it is a very rare man who doesn't want or expect sex reasonably soon in a dating relationship. Somehow the concept of a woman wanting/needing an emotional connection is elusive to nearly all the men I've gone out with. Is it that I tend to attract horn dogs? Or are there just more of them involved in Internet dating?

Is it that I tend to attract horn dogs?

The man who said he wanted a connection was unique. I hadn't encountered anyone like him. I asked him what made him have this point of view.

> "A lot of personal development work. I saw that in my past dating relationships I'd put too much emphasis on sex and pressed for it before I really knew the woman. We'd wake up next to each other a few months after beginning dating and realize we didn't really know if we had compatible values, goals, or beliefs. Our relationship was based mostly on sex. And I decided I wanted more."

I could have kissed him right then. But he was driving, so I saved it for later.

I'd heard there are men out there like this — in fact my male Adventures in Delicous Dating After 40 readers are, based on their comments. But to actually be dating one — I felt like I'd come upon a unicorn. Single men like this are rumored to be out there, but encountering one personally — what a treat.

Have you dated men who wanted a solid connection before becoming sexual? If so, how has that worked out?

Friends with benefits — yes or no?

An Adventures in Delicous Dating After 40 reader wrote:

> An attractive, charming and very-much-younger out-of-town male friend with whom I talk on the phone every few months for hours recently realized I have been celibate since deciding to divorce a few years ago.

> He was profoundly shocked and decided that on his next visit to my city he was taking me 'out on the town' rather than just dinner and talking, as we usually do on his visits. He implied strongly that he was perfectly willing to step up to friends with benefits (FWB) with no weirdness.

> A big part of me views sex as a commitment thing. Another part is starting to climb walls and have trouble sleeping.

> We have known each other for years, have always gotten along well and have many traits

in common, and he is a real knight-in-shin-ing-armor type.

So, why not? One reason — he's a lot younger than me — as in old enough to drink but only by a bit!

Is this a bad idea to accept the invite? Is it too likely to damage the friendship? Or him?

I am in DEEP water here, and would like some outside counsel. I need another female level head to make sense. My personal experience is just TOO limited in the dating arena (let alone the FWB one!) to have practical experience in this regard, and I knew you would be able to offer some perspective on the pros and cons based on the REAL world.

Dear Benefit-less Friend:

As you are wise enough to know, sex nearly always changes the dynamics, no matter how hard you try to make it not. Women let loose with that cuddling hormone, so they get more attached, even if intellectually we know it's just FWB.

> *"Don't use someone else's body to satisfy your own sexual needs."*

My mantra is, "Don't use someone else's body to satisfy your own sexual needs."

It just complicates life. So, like you, my bias is for some kind of commitment, even if it's just a commitment to be exclusive while you're sexual.

So, my suggestion is to thank him but not take him up on his offer. With the exception of male Delicous Dating After 40 readers, generally men have less emotional investment in sex than we do.

What do you think? Have you had experience with FWB and if so, was it worth it?

Is your attitude toward dating sex the same as diets?

You've decided to hold off sex with the guy you're dating until you both feel the relationship is solid. Yes, you've made this decision before, only to watch it crumble as you have been swept away physically by his predecessors. But this time it's different. You want to keep your word to yourself. You want to act congruently with your decisions, not allow yourself to be seduced — or to seduce — just because it feels good.

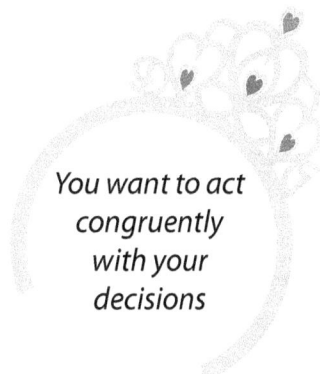

You want to act congruently with your decisions

Oh, no! You realize you've been approaching sex the same way you diet!

83

You start out with strong resolve, committing not to do anything that is counter to your stated goals. You vow to live in alignment with what you say you want (whether it's exercise regularly and limit sweets or exercise self-control and limit sweet, passionate kisses). You know it will take huge amounts of self-control, but you are determined this time to stick to your guns.

You're fine for a while, congratulating yourself on your fortitude and willpower. You feel good about yourself for showing such strong tenacity. But after a while you feel yourself vacillating. "What harm will a cookie or two (or fill in your own favorite seductive technique here) do? I can stop there. It will be fine."

And you've entered the slippery slope. You indulge. Then you beat yourself up mentally, chastising yourself like you'd never allow another person to talk to you. You work to recover, redoubling your efforts at staving off the forbidden fruit/activities. But your commitment has been damaged, if not broken. It is hard to keep depriving yourself of something you love.

Or perhaps you were able to rekindle your dedication to your goal and not give in to instant gratification. If so, you are not tempted by the delicious treats you know are in front of you. You feel great about being clear on what you want and not faltering.

No matter what your approach, do you see any parallels of dating sex and diets? (If you're one of those lucky people who've never been on a diet, welll, never mind!)

Does he know what turns you on?

oes the guy you're dating know what turns you on? Or does he make assumptions based on what turns him on?

Does he make assumptions based on what turns him on?

I received a bawdy video emailed from an old beau turned friend. It was clips of naked, buxom women playing various sports — gymnastics, calisthenics, etc. He thought it would turn me on.

I said, "It's a guy video."

"What do you mean?"

"Most of the women I know aren't turned on by naked women."

"What turns them on?"

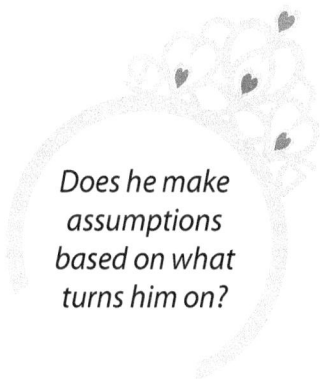

"Naked *MEN*! Good looking ones!"

Now wouldn't you think a 55-year-old man would know this, considering he was married for 10 years and has had many subsequent girlfriends in the last 20 years? Or did he go with women who were turned on by naked women? Or these past gals didn't tell him this didn't do it for them?

I think the lesson here is not to be afraid to tell your guy what gets you going — and what doesn't. The latter needs to be delivered gently, not angrily or condescendingly. But guy pals tell us over and over — men need clear instructions. They don't notice hints well. So let him know! You will both be much happier.

(I know you're thinking, "Does this explain why he's an ex-beau?")

"What would you need to feel comfortable having sex?"

I never would have thought of this question, but a friend suggested it as a way of discussing the desire to step up a dating relationship, without it just happening willy nilly in the heat of the moment. I pondered what I'd say if I were asked. Answers did not pour forth, but only came after some concerted thinking. Not that I've ever had a man come even remotely close to asking. If I have shared criteria in the past, guys typically try to talk me out of them.

Guys typically try to talk me out of my criteria

But I realize I'd never asked a man this question either. It has never seemed to be an issue, with most men rushing toward intimacy, so I imagine the answer would be "a willing woman." OK, maybe I'm a tad jaded.

I gathered up the courage to ask a man I'd been dating three months. He said, "I want to be in love with you." Wow! I'd never heard a man be so clear. I couldn't help think it sounded more like something a woman would say. (Yes, I know this is stereotypical.) We then discussed what we each needed to feel comfortable with various steps along the way. I agreed with nearly all of his and he mine.

It was refreshing to hear a man talk about taking our time, building a strong foundation first. He was aware of the ramifications and potential hurt caused by entering a sexual relationship before both parties are solidly connected. Of course, some people don't need that emotional connection, but he realized he does and that the women he's dated in the past have, so he's conscientious about it.

This conversation was so revealing and helpful that I've now added this question to my repertoire for after dating a guy for a while. And if he isn't able to come up with his criteria, I offer mine first so he knows I'm clear. There is less opportunity for persuading as he knows my boundaries and if he tries to dissuade me from them, it will tell me all I need to know about his respect — or lack thereof — for mine. And if I try to persuade him, I am disrespecting his values.

Have you asked anything similar to this? If so, how did it work? Do you have a different phrasing of the question?

When sexual electricity can scorch you

His smile ignites you. His touch sends currents up your spine. His kiss jolts you like you've been jump-started.

We dream — nay, fantasize — about this kind of sexual energy.

You are intoxicated by the charged feelings which blow the fuses of any rational thinking. You relish the feeling of the energy coursing through your body. It can be addicting, like a pyromaniac of passion. You're ablaze in ardor — or is it just lust? Probably.

You're ablaze in ardor — or is it just lust?

Yet if we've experienced it a few times, we also know it can scorch your heart when this sexual electricity surges too much too fast. Just like a bonfire can singe if you get too close for too long, your feelings can incinerate by burning too hot too quickly. Soon all that is left are embers — or worse, cold coals. And you wonder what happened to that once-blazing and romantic flame. Poof! Up in smoke.

Is it worth it to experience the red-hot fire of lust? If you don't delude yourself into thinking that this spark will be fueled more than a few hours, days, or weeks. It is if you know it is temporary heat — and your partner does too — it can be exhilarating. Yet most of us aren't able to be that detached, unplugging our emotions and tamping down hopes that this is kindling a long-term attraction.

But if you're lucky, you might be able to fan the flames of this passion fire for many years, maybe even decades. Some have. Maybe you two will be among the lucky ones.

Unfortunately, for most of us, this sexual inferno leaves us burnt out on love — at least for a little while as we salve our charred heart.

"I'm not just some girl you met on the Internet"

On the TV show "Private Practice" two colleagues decided to take their sexual chemistry to the "friends with benefits" level. However, when in the bedroom ready to commence, she couldn't go through with it, claiming that sex together would cheapen their relationship.

She exclaims, "I'm not just some girl you met on the Internet."

In other words, she's saying that Internet dating sites are the equivalent to hookup sites — prostitution without payment. Easy sex. Women who list themselves on the sites must be loose.

Hmmm.

I suppose this perception by some has made Internet dating seem tawdry to them, or just for the desperate with few other choices. For losers or the promiscuous.

This does explain, however, how quickly some men have come on to me. I am not a hot babe, wearing revealing come-hither attire. But some men have acted like first-date sex is the norm. Or even second-date sex.

Is it that the anonymity allows people to pursue their most basic needs — sex — with impunity? For many — especially those in midlife — Internet dating has replaced the bar scene. In their youth it might have been common to go to a club and hook up with someone for the night. Or for many, that's what their friends did, even if they weren't successful at it. So now instead of a bar, they have a drink date and see where it leads. They hope it leads to the bedroom, if enough drinks are imbibed. So what if he has to spring for a $50 dinner. What a small price for a quick roll in the hay! Less than a hooker and he didn't have to drive through the scary part of town.

Have you noticed that men you meet on the Internet have an expectation of sex earlier than men you meet through other methods? If so, why do you think the expectation is different?

Does dancing skill equal lovemaking prowess?

In "Dirty Dancing," we are seduced by Patrick Swayze's dance moves. He is so smooth, so sexy, so hot. We long for a man who moves like that, who is so sure of himself and knows how to move with us in perfect union. But was he as good in intimate situations as he was in public?

As we left the dance floor, a date stated that he could tell what kind of lover a woman was by how she danced. I was surprised at the comment, as I'd never heard it before. So I began comparing the dancing style of my former lovers.

However, I haven't danced with many of my sweeties, and I haven't made love with many dance partners. So that narrowed down the field for analysis. What could I tell about those who I'd experienced in both situations? Was my date right? Could I tell what kind of lover a man would be by how he danced?

There were some correlations. These are the characteristics that were discernible in both environments:

- ❤ Confidence (or shyness)

- ❤ Fun and laughter (or seriousness)

- ❤ Tenderness (or roughness)

- ❤ Sensitivity to partner's mood and needs (or insensitivity)

- ❤ Uninhibitedness (or reservedness)

- ❤ Generosity (or self-focus)

- ❤ Initiative (or lack thereof)

- ❤ Comfortable in his body, unembarrassed with how he moves, likes how movement feels (or self-conscious)

- ❤ Controlling (or allowing for ebb and flow between partners)

However, I'm sure there are many exceptions. Someone could be an excellent ballroom dancer, for example, and be too formulaic in bed. Or maybe someone is a great lover, but has two left feet on the dance floor. Some people perform better with an audience and some worse.

What's your experience? Have you had great lovers who were also great dancers? Or was one experience much better than the other?

How dating sex is like waffles

It can be hot, steamy and mouth watering. With a great recipe and tasty condiments, it can be delectable.

But just as with the first waffle, the first time with a new love can also be anemic and unsatisfying. In fact, many midlife daters report the initial romp to be less fulfilling than they hoped, even when it is with someone with whom they are emotionally and physically excited.

The initial romp to be less fulfilling than they hoped

So do what you do with the first waffle — throw it out!

Does that mean to ignore the first time exploring bedroom bliss with your sweetie? Not really. But it does mean not putting a lot of weight on the outcome. You are learning about each other, what the other likes, communicating what you want. There can be a lot of pressure. So if one or both of you don't reach nirvana, it is not a pronouncement that you are sexually incompatible. It means that this part of your relationship is a work in progress, just like other parts.

With waffles, you expect the first one to be "practice." Keep that same attitude toward your first-time intimacy with your beau. And, just like with waffles, give the "iron" (your connection) time to heat up so the subsequent attempts yield more satisfying results.

When I make waffles, some of the batter oozes out the side. My waffles aren't always beautiful to behold — but they are usually yummy if I put the love and attention into them that is needed to have a scrumptious repast. Your first (or second) intimate encounter can be inelegant. But given the right ingredients (mutual respect, communication, desire, humor), horizontal happiness is bound to be cooked up.

Proof that men lose common sense when aroused

You are probably thinking, "Who needs proof that men lose their ability to think when they are aroused?" We know this anecdotally, and men will agree, so we're not man bashing. But in his book *Predictably Irrational* author Dan Ariely cites a study he conducted that gives us empirical evidence.

Dr. Ariely recruited 35 college men to answer questions about their responses to sexual stimuli and activities in a non-aroused state, then again in an aroused state. Each participant was asked to

1) "evaluate the attractiveness of different sexual stimuli and activities,

2) the lengths the respondent would go to in order to obtain sexual gratification, and

3) their attitude toward sexual risks in the heat of passion."

The sad part for me was the dramatic difference between the subjects' answers in the different states. In an aroused state, the men said they were much more likely to:

- take a date to a fancy restaurant to increase his chance of having sex with her

- tell a woman that he loved her to increase the chance that she would have sex with him

- encourage his date to drink to increase the chance that she would have sex with him

- keep trying to have sex after his date says "no."

- slip a woman a drug to increase the chance that she would have sex with him.

Additionally, the men said they were less likely to use a condom in the aroused state if even if they didn't know the sexual history of a new sexual partner. And they were also less likely to use a condom if they were afraid that a woman might change her mind while he went to get it.

Since this study was done on college-aged men, what does it mean for us?

Since this study was done on college-aged men, what does it mean for us? Presumably, midlife men have more maturity and common sense than an 18 to 22 year old. So is this data relevant or not?

I can only share my experience having gone out now with 93 midlife men. While I'd say they are less driven sexually than college-aged men, many midlife men still have a strong sexual drive. So much so that when aroused they can lose much of their sense of appropriateness. I've had men who have said, "I can wait as long as you need before we have sex" then try to press forward after I told them I wasn't ready. I've had men ignore boundaries that we set when we were sitting across the dinner table an hour earlier. I chocked it up to their being horny, disrespectful, and single focused.

The study says both men and women need to avoid getting into situations where men are likely to ignore their own boundaries and monitors. It said you need to not get into situations that would test them. Yes, some men can manage to pull themselves out of a passionate fervor, but some just don't seem to have that control. It's as if a stun gun has been shot into their brain and it is numb. A common phrase I hear from men is, "We can only think with one brain at time — either the one in our head or the one in our …."

So the bottom line for us is if we know we are not ready to become sexual with a man, don't get into situations where our own passion can meld into theirs. I know it sounds common sense, but as Dr. Ariely has shown empirically, common sense gets run over by the Mac truck called lust.

Too-soon seduction: "I'm special, but not THAT special"

My pal shared his counter-stereotypical challenge: Women tried to seduce him before he felt the relationship merited it. Most of my dating men friends have shared they were ready for sex much sooner than the women they dated. Therefore I knew this pal was a rarity worth studying.

So I probed.

He explained that when a woman tries to get him to "go horizontal" on the first, second, or third date, he feels it's too soon. The common thread is she tells him she never gets sexual this early in a relationship, but he is special. Thus his comment to me that he knows he's special, but not that special so as to cause a supposedly discerning woman to abandon her hard-won wisdom to hold off on sex until in a solid relationship. He knows they haven't created the bond that is needed for sex to be anything but manipulative or a romp, neither of which interests him. He surmises that she is easy and uses the "you're special" comment to justify her looseness.

Some women, he explained, have tried to use their womanly wiles to advance the relationship physically before it has adequately developed emotionally. He knows this is sure trouble if he allows physical urges to trump the slower progressing emotional and intellectual ones. He's clear this takes time, not something that happens within a few dates — or even a few weeks.

While he understands that there can be instant chemistry and/or mutual physical needs, he's experienced enough to know that giving into these desires too early nearly always causes upset. You really don't know the person, and sex generally changes everything unless you're both only into a short-term fling. More often than not, one party gets attached and expectations change once you go horizontal.

One party gets attached and expectations change once you go horizontal

He was not boasting, but lamenting when he shared that he's had to stop women from dragging him into the bedroom, or undressing him, or doing a strip tease for him after only a date or two. You'd think he looks like a Chippendale, but he doesn't! He is intelligent, articulate, educated, confident, respectful, and funny, but not what we would consider a classic hunk. He knows that the woman's behavior telegraphs her loneliness, neediness or horniness, and has little to do with his appeal.

Luckily, I've rarely been in the "this is special between us" place and abandoned my criteria to take it slow. When I have, just like my friend, the results have been disastrous, leaving much unhappiness in the wake of the tryst.

So I was glad he shared his perspective that a mature, emotionally grounded man thinks too-soon seduction is a problem, not a godsend. For while he's a sexy and sensual man, he isn't so sex obsessed that he forgets the havoc that can be left when sex enters the picture too soon. It reminded me that there really are midlife men who are interested in long-term satisfaction, not short-term gratification. Thank heavens!

If having sex meant you were married

I attended a lovely Jewish wedding last weekend. The bride was resplendent and the groom handsome as they stood under the chupah in front of the rabbi (the bride's father) and the cantor (her god-father). Outside at sunset, the family and friends stood encircling the couple on the grass. The cantor's sweet singing, including a song he wrote for the bride, soared in the crisp evening air. Candle luminaria lit the lawn on which we all stood, and a lone guitarist strummed entrance and exit music.

I'd arrived early, and my friend (the bride's mother), showed me and another couple the quaint sleeping rooms in the inn where the ceremony and celebration were held. In showing me the bridal suite, she mentioned that in traditional or Biblical Jewish tradition, when a couple has sex they are then considered married.

Wow!

I spewed out, "Crap! How many men would I be married to then? And can I get alimony?"

But my smart-aleck-ness aside, it made think how we would approach dating sex differently if doing the act meant we were then married.

Sex – even in midlife – has a broad spectrum of acceptability. One study in the UK showed half the over-40 dating

How would approach dating sex differently if doing the act meant we were then married?

women said they'd be willing to have sex on the first date. Others, like Steve Harvey, say no sex for 3 months. Some people won't have sex until engagement or marriage. I'm not here to tell you what you should do.

But imagine how you might shift your feelings about when to have sex if doing it meant you were married to the man. That would certainly put the kibosh on booty calls and casual sex.

Thinking of sex with this gravity makes me realize there are very few men with whom I would have been intimate. It puts a whole new spin on the significance of sex.

How would you have led your life differently if having sex meant you were then married? How would it affect how you date now?

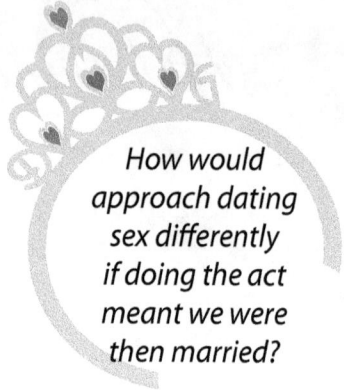

Would you be happy with a cuddle buddy?

There are various types of "buddies" in dating. Some you're good with; others you're not. You don't really want a no-strings-attached sex-only relationship. You want some strings if you are going to get intimate — at least some interest in exploring if you both want there to be strings, not just "That was fun. See you later."

You crave tender touching and caresses, but there's no one on the horizon that interests you enough to go down the physically intimate path. So you seem caught between no physicality at one extreme to enduring a booty call just to get some physical contact.

Enter the concept of cuddle buddy. "What's that?" you ask. Good question, as I just invented the term, although the concept has been around. It's where two people (of the opposite sex for this blog's discussion) who are fond of each other but never got into a dating relationship. They enjoy each other's company and like to hang out. But there's a deal breaker for one or both of them that prevented the relationship from getting intimate.

Neither of you is dating anyone else so you don't get your skin hunger satisfied elsewhere. So when you sit on the couch watching a movie, you end up smack next to each other. His arm may go around her shoulders, her head may rest on his chest. One may rest a hand on the other's leg. There is no kissing, just cuddling. They may even fall asleep on the couch this way.

A cuddle buddy is only good when you both understand there is no interest in going further. If one of you breaks the invisible wall and starts kissing or trying to advance, it all falls apart. One of you has to stop the other and there is an awkwardness between you then. Or maybe the other doesn't stop and things go beyond where you both know you should, and then it becomes really strange. Now you are lovers, but you don't really want to be this person's lover because of the aforementioned deal breaker. Do you "break up" even though you were really never going together? Or do you try to ignore it hoping things will go back to normal? Or do you talk about it to clear the air, but things really don't go back the way they were?

So try cuddle buddying only when you believe you're both clear on the boundaries and are willing to live within them. But it is a nice alternative to the other kinds of dating buddies.

Have you had this kind of relationship? If so, was it easy or hard to maintain your boundaries? What happened when one of you met a romantic partner? How did it end — or did it?

Arbitrary sexual time line

Three dates.

One month.

Ten dates.

Three months.

I've heard all these as people's criteria for when to first get intimate with a new love.

A pal recently shared that he has been taken aback by some women's arbitrary time line for intimacy. He once dated a woman who, on their 4-month anniversary, announced it was time for them to have sex — that night! They did. He said it felt mechanical because they hadn't built the emotional connection that he sought to make it fulfilling.

Do you have such a time line? Or do you just have certain parameters, like "never on a first date," or "whenever it feels right"?

I don't have suggestions for when you "should" get naked with your sweetie for the first time. I've learned

I need to feel a significant emotional connection, not just a physical one. And I need to trust that he won't just disappear afterwards — not that there needs to be a spoken commitment. A pledge of exclusivity is important, although I've had that with a past beau and he still cheated on me.

The important thing is for you to know what you need to proceed to this step in the relationship. An arbitrary time line isn't usually enough. You could date someone for months and still not have the emotional connection you feel you need. However, I would be skeptical if you say you have a significant enough emotional connection after just a week or so. That's usually the brain's chemicals tricking you into thinking you have more than is likely after such a short time. So even if you feel that you are soul mates by the end of week two, an arbitrary wait period of, say a month, then would be wise. A lot can happen in those ensuing two weeks.

> *The important thing is for you to know what you need*

Some experts suggest 3 months is long enough for a man to show his true self and for you to see him without his best wooing self put forward. My experience corroborates this. Usually by 90 days, the chinks in his armor begin to show and you can see if you can live with those or not. So before you've gotten physically entwined, you have a better sense of the man. Because once you share horizontal happiness, the relationship usually shifts dramatically. As the aforementioned pal expressed, "The flood gates of expectations open and a man can drown in what rushes forth unabated."

Yes, we women generally do have expectations once whoopee has been made. That is if we didn't perceive the encounter as just a fling. So we need to see that the man is someone we're interested in being with and he's shown he's interested in being with us.

So examine your own criteria. Ask yourself why you have determined that you would be ready to have sex at a certain point. You may stick to those boundaries, or you may decide they are really just arbitrary. If the latter, make a list of what you need to feel comfortable before becoming intimate.

Sex, ED, and the single midlife woman

long-time reader asked me to address a sensitive, yet not uncommon midlife dating issue — middle-aged sex and erectile dysfunction.

He asks, "How do you handle an attempt at sex that doesn't work? How do you decide if this is a man you want to continue to see or is this a red flag?"

Can we talk? We are adults so we're going to use adult words.

There is lots written about Viagra and ED, but what I've read is mostly written for long-time partners where there is a strong bond and, one would hope, a willingness to discuss this sort of thing and find a solution that works for both parties.

However, in dating, even after dating a while, there may not be that bond. Which then complicates the matter.

Men, in my experience, equate their masculinity to their ability to satisfy their woman in bed. (Or at least to do what he thinks satisfies his woman, whether it actually does or not.) In fact, some women feel similarly — if a man can't satisfy her in bed, he's not fully a man, even if he takes care of the family financially, contributes equally to family chores, is active in family activities, and otherwise shows he's an emotionally mature partner.

So a man's ability to perform in bed takes on enormous weight — sometimes for both partners.

If he has some instances of ED there is more pressure. He knows he may not be able to get or keep an erection. He feels like a failure. He may blame the woman for not being sexy enough, or for not trying to arouse him, even though she has done her "job" in these areas previously. A beau broke up with me soon after his inability to perform. I got the impression he blamed me for this, even though I tried to be supportive.

So they go in search of the magic pill — this time a blue one. They think this will suddenly make him an unquenchable sex machine. After all the commercials say something about erections lasting more than 4 hours — "Think of all the fun we could have in 4 hours!" one or both of them fanaticize.

What they don't know is that the blue pill works with some men and not others. A former beau told me he had ED and so we tried Viagra. Didn't work. My beau felt like a horrible failure. It really affected his self-esteem.

Also, it's expensive. The aforementioned DG reader said he bought a 10-pill prescription for $220! So it's the price of a movie for the two of you. Not too bad, unless your $22 habit is every day and you are out of a job right now.

Both parties seem to expect miracles. One or both of them think he just pops it and within minutes he has his 19-year-old libido back. Well, it doesn't increase desire. It doesn't cause an erection. All it does is allow more blood to flow into the penis, but a man still needs

Both parties seem to expect miracles.

to feel aroused. In many cases Viagra is needed simply because there has been vascular damage and blood flow is diminished.

Some men wonder if a women might think if he needs Viagra to have sex, he isn't attracted to her. If a woman is astute, she understands the biology of the situation. If she isn't, she may take it personally and feel he's not into her enough for her to arouse him without the aid.

So what to do if you're dating someone who isn't able to perform? If you are connected enough to attempt the horizontal tango, you should be connected enough to talk about it sensitively and supportively. Tell him you know this is uncomfortable for most men

and you wouldn't mind at all experimenting with some pharmaceutical aid. If appropriate, offer to split the cost, although be careful as some men will find that adding insult to injury. So know your man before offering and don't if you think he'll be even more humiliated.

This would also be a great time to bring up your own needs, if you haven't yet. Midlife women often need help to either get in the mood or make the experience more satisfying. Speak up so he knows he's not the only one who could use some other aids.

This discussion will most likely bring you closer together. If it doesn't and he gets defensive or goes poof, oh well. You've saved yourself from further involvement with a man who's not emotionally mature enough to talk about solutions to issues around aging. You don't want to spend another nanosecond of your precious time with someone like that.

What's your no-kissing zone?

At the train station in Cheshire, England, officials erected a "No Kissing" sign since traffic stacked up while amorous lovers made out bidding each other good-bye.

It made me wonder about our own personal no-kissing zones. Although many (most?) daters don't mind some PDA, there are places we'd rather not neck.

For example, after several weeks of intensive calls, an out-of-town suitor decided he just couldn't wait to show me how glad he was to be with me at last. As we walked to the restaurant down my home town main drag, he backed me up to a building and started necking. While I appreciated his attraction to me, I was dismayed at his choice of spots, as who knew which of my clients might amble by.

I tried to break off to tell him to wait until we were in private, but he scoffed saying, "I don't care who sees." Thanks, bub, for caring about my desires!

With other men, I was less concerned with being

smooched in public. While I try to balance honoring spontaneity with discretion, if besotted with a man I didn't mind long smooches outside a neighborhood haunt, no matter who was around.

In fact, one of my most delicious dates was at the movies with a particularly alluring sweetheart. We chose an early movie with few people in the theater and sat in the very back. We started canoodling, conscious of being as quiet as possible. We did nothing more than kiss. A few rows in front of us sat another middle-aged couple. At the end of the flick, they turned to look at us and seemed shocked we weren't teenagers.

However, that was in the dark, not broad daylight, and not in a place where others would easily see us.

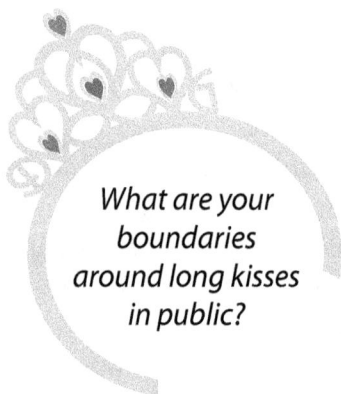

What are your boundaries around long kisses in public?

What are your boundaries around long kisses (not just quick pecks) in public? Does it depend on who you're with and your feelings toward him? Or the location — neighborhood vs. unfamiliar area? Or the amount of wine you've had?

Casual sex

His online profile mentioned that he loved sex, something that is usually a yellow flag as it says the man doesn't have much of an appropriateness filter. But other things he shared made me give him some slack.

Half an hour into our first phone call, he said he "loved, loved, loved sex." He suggested our first date be at his house to watch a move and if I wanted, stay over. I said I wasn't comfortable going to a strange man's house on the first date. I should have called it quits then, but I'd enjoyed most other aspects of our conversation.

Before we met, during our second call, he mentioned the previous Saturday night he was with a woman he used to date from Match.com. "I ended up staying the night" he shared. He now wanted to get together with me.

It was clear his attitude about sex was different than mine. He obviously felt no need or desire to be exclusive with someone with whom he was having sex, since he was trying to set up a date with me.

He asked if I wanted to get together. While I appreciated his candor, I didn't want to get involved with someone who I felt I'd be fighting off throughout the evening because he clearly was only interested in one thing. And if we were to start seeing each other, I couldn't trust that if we became intimate he'd be exclusive.

Is casual sex bad? Not between two people who have the same goals, are open about them and are responsible. But it's not for me.

So I was grateful he laid out his hand so clearly and so soon. It saved me a lot of time and headache.

Have you gone out with someone who clearly wanted only casual sex when you wanted more?

Your naivete can hurt you

A friend shared that she was too naive after her decades-long marriage ended. She was clueless about not only how to be with men other than her now-ex-husband, but about how she could be harmed while she learned

She was clueless about how to be with men.

Soon after her divorce, she started dating a successful man and they had regular make-out sessions. One day, he said he had a cold sore on his lip. Her mother had always referred to canker sores as cold sores, so she didn't know the difference or think anything about it.

A few weeks later, she got a cold and was constantly blowing her nose. She felt an odd tingling under her nose which blistered and festered. She'd never had anything like this so had no idea what it was. But she was too busy to go to the doctor, so she covered it the best she could with makeup.

Months later it happened again. It seemed to be re-lated to colds, so she finally asked her doctor. She was horrified to learn it was herpes simplex virus. While the doctor said 50%-80% of adults carry the virus, many never get the sores. So she could have already had the virus in her system — or she could have received it from her then-beau.

I've heard many midlife daters say they don't use condoms because they trust their partner. They don't insist on an STD test before going condom-free. Some say, "I'm not dating a drug addict." But today I heard a report that said 25% of those infected with HIV don't know it.

So am I saying no kissing while dating? Kissing is a fun part of dating. But my friend has now vowed to slow down physical contact that can carry surprises. While you can insist on having STD tests before getting intimate, it would be awkward to ask if your date ever gets cold sores.

If cold sores aren't part of your history, investigate what to look for in an outbreak in others so you can make sure to not touch the infected area. And the virus can become genital herpes through physical contact, so no matter how tempting, best to lay off any kissing or intimacy while one of you has an outbreak.

Resources

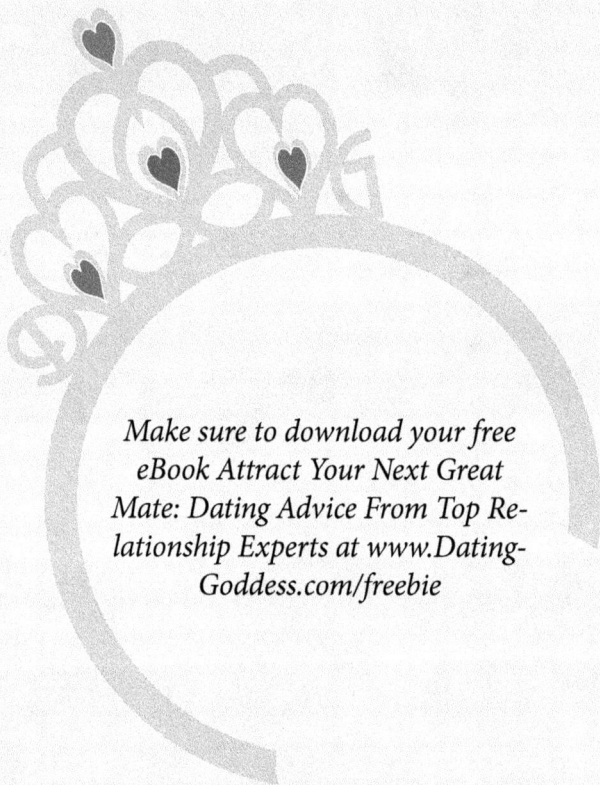

Make sure to download your free eBook Attract Your Next Great Mate: Dating Advice From Top Relationship Experts at www.Dating-Goddess.com/freebie

Afterword

At the time of this writing, I have not yet found my true King Charming. I continue my search with verve. I've become more discerning about what I want and don't want. I've met some wonderful men pals — my treasures — who continue to be in touch.

I wish you much luck in your adventure. It will be fun and frustrating, exhilarating and exasperating, and sexy or sexless. So much depends on you, your approach and your attitude. My books are designed to help you enjoy as much as possible and ward off unpleasantness. But nearly all adventures have wonderful highs as well as a few lows. If you know that going in and arm yourself with information on what to expect, you'll have more of the positives and fewer of the negatives.

Please drop by www.DatingGoddess.com and join in the discussion and report on your experiences.

Dating Goddess

Resources

o to www.datinggoddess.com to access a variety of useful resources. We work to suggest resources we think have value.

Dating and relationship book reviews

These reviews will save you time and money as I've given you my take on specific books, CDs and more. Some are worth your effort to buy and read or listen to them — some are not. We're always adding new book reviews, so check frequently. We'll also notify our mailing list when new resources are added.

Dating site links

There are a lot of dating sites on the Internet. I've listed the ones I think are worth investigating.

Dating products and tools

Dating can be daunting. We're continually looking at

ways to make it easier and more fun. We'll provide info on games, tools, even date-wear that will help others know you're available, or help you get to know potential suitors better.

Dating and relationship advice sites

Advice "experts" abound on the Internet as anyone can self-proclaim themseves as expert — even if they haven't dated in 30 years and never in midlife. I've worked to find experts who's advice I generally think is solid.

Midlife recources

We'll feature Web sites, books, events and other resources we think might interest you.

Newly discovered resources

I'll add other resources as we discover them, subscribe to our mailing list to get the scoop as soon as we find them. Go to www.DatingGoddess.com to register for our mailing list. Don't worry, we won't sell or give your email to anyone.

Acknowledgments

Let me start by acknowledging the 112 men who helped trigger the lessons contained in this book. Some prompted several! They remain nameless here to protect their identity, although most would recognize references to them. Plus the thousands more whose winks, emails and calls didn't result in a date, but helped me learn the dating game. And all those men who I emailed who never responded — such a blessing to have them weed themselves out.

> I acknowledge the 112 men who triggered my lessons

I'd like to thank my Seven Sisters mastermind group for the tremendous brainstorming, noodling, strategizing and encouragement. I wouldn't have begun this project without the prodding of Val Cade, Chris Clarke-Epstein, Mariah Burton Nelson, Sue Dyer, Sam Horn and Marilynn Mobley.

Thank you to my good friends who've listened to my dating stories ad nauseam, and whose support and wisdom are embedded in this text. Ed Betts, Ken Braly, Bruce Daley, Tom Drews, Elaine Floyd, Paulette Ensign, Scott Friedman, Craig Harrison, Mary Jansen, Tom Johnson, Sandy Jones, Mary Kilkenny, Ellie Klevins, Patrick Lynch, Mary Marcdante, Barbara McNichol, Ann Peterson, Anthony Ramsey, Caterina Rando, Kristy Rogers, Jana Stanfield, Holly Steil, Terry Tepliz, and George Walther, thank you.

The Adventures in Delicious Dating After 40 series

The *Adventures in Delicious Dating After 40* series is designed to help you understand your own midlife dating journey. It is not a road map, as we all take different routes. It is a guide to help you understand yourself, midlife men, and the dating process. Hopefully, you'll not only learn from the lessons and insights shared in this series, but you'll examine how they apply — or don't — to your own dating adventure.

You'll get the scoop on what you need to know, what's changed since you last dated, and how to navigate inevitable bumps in the road.

Following is an overview of each book in the series and a sampling of some of the chapter titles. All are detailed at www.DatingGoddess.com.

Date or Wait: Are You Ready for Mr. Great?

Are you ready for a special man in your life? You have a great life. But you know you'd like a special man to share it. You think you're ready to date, but you haven't done it in a while.

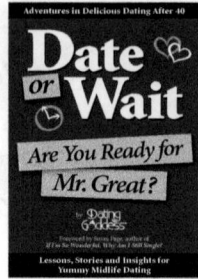

What should you consider before you actually start dating full bore? Even if you've reentered the dating world, this will give you a foundation of attitude and philosophy to make your adventure more fulfilling.

Sample chapters

🩶 From hurt to flirt

🩶 Dating is like Baskin-Robbins

🩶 You've got to kiss a lot of…princes!

🩶 What's your definition of dating success?

🩶 Are you open to receiving?

🩶 Dating: A self-designed personal-growth workshop

🩶 Hands-on dating research

🩶 Being present to the presents

🩶 Being aggressively single

🩶 Approaching dating like a buffet

🩶 Is Brad Pitt ruining your love life?

🩶 Treasures can come in dented packages

Assessing Your Assets: Why You're A Great Catch

You have many wonderful quali- ties. But it's easy to focus on one's flaws — at least what seem like flaws to you. However, to the right man your im- perfections are endearing, attractive and lovable. You have to be clear what you offer a man who will find you enchanting.

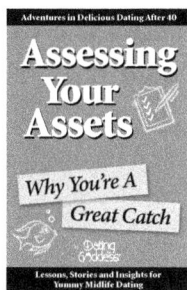

Assessing Your Assets helps you look at what you bring to a new relationship. It will help you see your good points so you'll approach dating with more confidence.

Sample chapters

💜 Don't think you are damaged goods

💜 You are (probably) more attractive than you think!

💜 They aren't called "hate handles"

💜 Are you a good man picker?

💜 What are your deal breakers?

💜 Are you arguing your limitations?

💜 Turn your liabilities into assets

💜 The strong vs. nice woman debate

💜 Is your sense of humor stunting your dating?

💜 Why are we drawn to bad boys?

💜 The zest test

In Search of King Charming: Who Do I Want to Share My Throne?

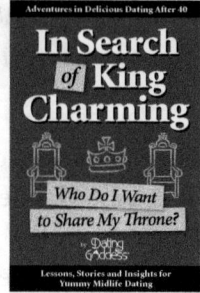

You are no longer looking for "Prince" Charming because you are a queen. You want someone who is at your level, not groveling at your feet. You want a king — someone who's your equal and with whom you can rule the throne together!

This book focuses on helping you better define what you want beyond tall, dark and handsome! You'll consider characteristics you might not have thought of before. You'll look at what you want now.

Sample chapters

💜 Building your Franken-boyfriend

💜 What's your "perfect boyfriend's" job description?

💜 A man to go with your wardrobe

💜 In search of the elusive good kisser

💜 When you're clear on what you want, it appears

💜 Are you dating the same guy in different bodies?

💜 Does he fit in your world?

💜 What's your kissing quotient?

💜 Is your guy's loving muscle strong?

💜 Do you both have the same dating rhythm?

Embracing Midlife Men:
Insights Into Curious Behaviors

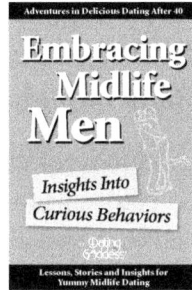

Do you sometimes scratch your head after interacting with a midlife man, wondering, "What could he possibly be thinking?" Especially if it's before, during or after a date with a man who presumably wants to impress you!

This book focuses on better understanding midlife men's behaviors. When you grasp what's going on in his head it's much easier to embrace him. Men are wondrous creatures, so we need to understand them better and love them for who they are.

Sample chapters

💚 Men are like shoes

💚 Why men disappear when it gets serious

💚 Chivalry isn't dead —but it seems to be hibernating

💚 Do men want feisty women?

💚 Midlife men have forgotten how to date

💚 Are you getting prime time from your man?

💚 When a man tells you what he paid for things

💚 Does he treat you like his ex?

💚 Has Greg Behrendt done women a disservice?

💚 Tales of woo

Dipping Your Toe in the Dating Pool: Dive In Without Belly Flopping

You've decided you are ready — you want to start dating. Maybe you've already had a few coffee dates with several men. You want to be as successful as possible on your dating adventure.

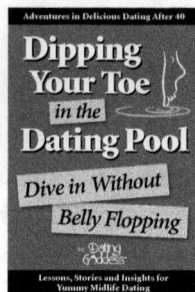

This book focuses on getting started on your dating adventures. We cover what you need to know as you begin your journey.

Sample chapters

💜 Do you have the right datewear?

💜 Dating with integrity

💜 Building your rejection muscle

💜 When "be yourself" is questionable advice

💜 Faux beaus and practice dating

💜 Are you making bad decisions out of loneliness?

💜 Being "in wonder" about your date's behavior

💜 When do you feel most vulnerable in dating?

💜 Are you out of his league — or he yours?

💜 Why listening is so seductive

Winning at the Online Dating Game: Stack the Deck in Your Favor

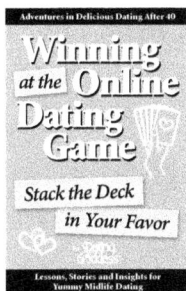

Internet dating can be frustrating or fruitful. It will be much less exasperating if you know how to read and weed out men's profiles that aren't appropriate for you. And you'll have a steady stream of potential suitors if you know how to write a compelling profile for yourself.

This book focuses on the ins and outs of online dating. How to play the game, which has it's own rules and language. If you don't understand how online dating works, you'll waste a lot of time connecting with men who are not a possible fit for you.

Sample chapters

♥ Shopping for men

♥ Safe online dating

♥ Is 21st Century dating unnatural?

♥ What do men look at in your profile?

♥ Euphemisms uncovered

♥ Are you describing yourself compellingly?

♥ No, I will not be dating your Harley

♥ Playing the online dating game

♥ Scantily clothed pictures

Check Him Out Before Going Out: Avoiding Dud Dates

Under the cloak of the anonymity that email and the phone provides, men often reveal more than they intend. If you ask the right questions you can find out a lot about his values and view of the world after just an interaction or two.

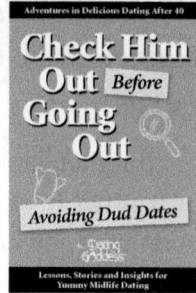

This book focuses on what you need to ask before agreeing to even a coffee date. You need to vet the men who email and call you to ensure you're not likely to waste your time with men who clearly aren't a match.

Sample chapters

💜 Becoming smitten with the fantasy

💜 Can Google help — or hinder — your dating life?

💜 Qualify your potential dates before meeting

💜 The art of consideration

💜 Anticipating a big date is like awaiting Santa

💜 Being seduced by what he is over who he is

💜 Are you his spare?

💜 My boyfriend, whom I haven't met

💜 When canceling is the right thing to do

💜 Politics, religion and sex — oh my!

First-Rate First Dates: Increasing the Chances of a Second Date

You can tell a lot about someone within the first 30 minutes. What does he talk about? Does he ask you questions? If so, what does he want to know about you? What do you need to know about him? How does he treat you? How does he treat those around you?

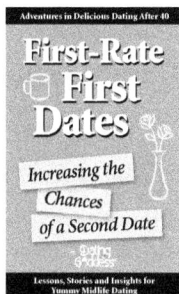

This book focuses on what goes on during the first date. How do you determine if you want a second date? What you can do to increase the likelihood your date will ask you for a second? That is if you want a repeat!

Sample chapters

💚 Start with coffee

💚 How do you greet him?

💚 When it clicks, throw out some of your criteria

💚 Tracking your date's score

💚 Clues a guy is just looking for a booty call

💚 12 signs he won't be asking for a second date

💚 First-date red flags that this guy isn't for you

💚 Honesty is not always the best policy

💚 Chemistry, or does he make my toes curl?

💚 Women's first-date blunders

Real Deal or Faux Beau: Should You Keep Seeing Him?

You've begun to go out with a man you like. How do you decide if you should continue seeing him, or if you should release him because he's not The One?

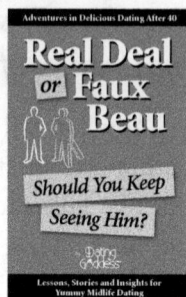

This book focuses on second dates and beyond. During the dating process you are both assessing if you want to keep seeing each other. This book helps you determine what questions you need to ask yourself.

Sample chapters

🩶 Deciding to see him again or not

🩶 What's your date's Delight/Disappointment Scale score?

🩶 Broaching tough conversations

🩶 "I want to respect me in the morning"

🩶 Does he invite you to his place?

🩶 Are you stingy in dating?

🩶 When his hand is on your knee too soon

🩶 Easy way to ask hard questions

🩶 Rose-colored glasses obscure red flags

🩶 If his stories don't add up, subtract yourself

Multidating Responsibly: Play the Field Without Being A Player

Playing the field is frowned on in some circles. There are definitely appropriate and inappropriate ways to date several men simultaneously.

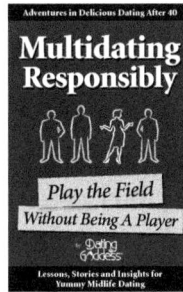

This book focuses on how to date around responsibly and with integrity without leading men on. If you do it with honesty, you can date several people at once until you're both ready to focus only on each other.

Sample chapters

💜 "Pimpin'" — Dating multiple guys

💜 Multi-dating pros and cons

💜 Your Date-A-Base — tracking multiple suitors

💜 "Hot bunking" your beaus

💜 Are you a "Let's Make a Deal" type of dater?

💜 Assume there are other women

💜 Dating's revolving door

💜 How long do you hedge your bet?

💜 Beware of multi-tasking when multi-dating

💜 Back burner beaus

💜 The boyfriend phone

Moving On Gracefully: Break Up Without Heartache

"Breaking up" sounds so high school, doesn't it? But part of the dating process is saying something when one of you decides not to date the other anymore. Going "poof" is not a mature or respectful option in midlife.

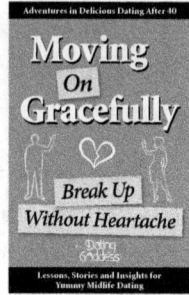

This book focuses on surviving a breakup, whether you initiate it or not. Either way, it's never easy to break up if you have developed any fondness toward the other.

Sample chapters

💜 Hello — goodbye: How to say no thanks after meeting

💜 Releasing back into the dating pool

💜 50 ways to leave your lover? 4 ways not to leave your suitor

💜 Breaking up is hard to do — right

💜 Why men go "poof"

💜 How to trump being dumped

💜 When breaking up is a "Get Out of Jail Free" card

💜 How to detect the end is near

💜 Failed relationships' blessings

💜 He's broken up with you — he just didn't tell you

💜 Rejection is protection

From Fear to Frolic: Get Naked Without Getting Embarrassed

This book focuses on what you need to consider and know before getting physically intimate with a man you're dating. This is nerve-wracking to many midlife women. This book will prepare you.

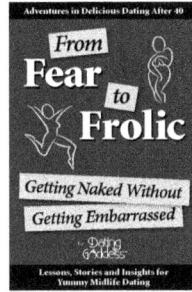

Sample chapters

💜 Sleepover do's and don'ts

💜 Does he want in your life — or just in your bedroom?

💜 Getting naked with him the first time

💜 An excuse to seduce or how important is bedroom bliss?

💜 What to ask yourself before getting naked with him

💜 Are you and your guy on the same sexual time line?

💜 Sharing your sexual owner's manual with him

💜 What women need from a man before having sex

💜 Why too-soon midlife sex is like non-fat food

💜 How dating sex is like waffles

💜 Too-soon seduction: "I'm special, but not THAT special"

Ironing Out Dating Wrinkles: Work Through Challenges Without Getting Steamed

Nearly all relationships have some ups and downs. Part of getting to know someone is knowing how they work through relationship misunderstandings.

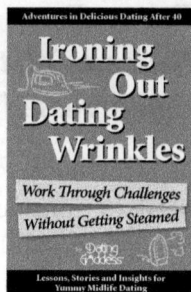

This book focuses on how to work through the inevitable hiccups that happen when you are getting to know each other. If you can both deal with challenges, the bond deepens and you find yourself smitten.

Sample chapters

- ♥ When your guy vexes you, ask what your highest self would do

- ♥ The first fight

- ♥ You want boo; he wants boo-ty

- ♥ Where's the line between getting your needs met and being selfish?

- ♥ Expressing your upset with your guy

- ♥ Is his toothbrush in your cabinet too soon?

- ♥ Do you love how he loves you?

- ♥ Is he collecting data on how to make you happy?

- ♥ Be careful of being smitten

- ♥ Exclusivity: How and when to broach it